MCAT Verbal, Quantitative, and Research Methods

COMPLETE STRATEGY REVIEW FOR THE MCAT

NextStep
TEST PREP nextsteptestprep.com

Printed in the United States of America

Second Printing, 2018

ISBN 978-1-944-935-22-1

Next Step Test Prep, LLC
4256 N Ravenswood Ave
Suite 207
Chicago IL 60613

www.nextsteptestprep.com

Revision Number: 1.2 (2018-04-01)

FREE ONLINE FULL LENGTH MCAT

Want to see how you would do on the MCAT
and understand where you need to focus your prep?

TAKE OUR FREE MCAT DIAGNOSTIC EXAM
and **FREE FULL LENGTH**
Timed practice that simulates Test Day and provides
comprehensive analysis, reporting, and in-depth explanations.

Included with this free account is the first lesson
in Next Step's online course, a free sample
from our science QBank, and more!

All of these resources are provided free to students who have
purchased a Next Step book. Register for your free account at:

http://nextsteptestprep.com/mcat-diagnostic

This page left intentionally blank.

TABLE OF CONTENTS

This page left intentionally blank.

How to Prepare for the MCAT

CHAPTER 1

0. Introduction

Welcome to the beginning of your MCAT prep journey! You've got a long road ahead of you, but Next Step will be there with you, helping you at each step along the way. Preparing for the MCAT begins with marshaling your resources and then setting out a plan for how best to use them.

The first thing to do is sign up for the free online prep bundle at Next Step's website here: https://nextsteptestprep.com/mcat-resources-page/. This bundle includes a free diagnostic test, science content diagnostic, full length exam, sample videos, and more. Next, create an account on Next Step's MCAT forums here: http://forum.nextstepmcat.com/. These forums allow you to ask questions of Next Step tutors and other students. Our faculty regularly put helpful blog posts up on the forums and answer questions relating to content, strategy, study schedules, and everything else MCAT-related. Finally, you need to make an account with the AAMC at AAMC.org. The official AAMC prep resources are an essential component of good prep, and you can purchase those directly from the AAMC (note if you've signed up for a Next Step online class or tutoring package, the AAMC resources are bundled in automatically).

Once you've registered, you need to put together resources to cover three aspects of MCAT preparation: content review, practice passages, and simulated Full Lengths. The easiest way to do this is to sign up for an MCAT course, as the Next Step course includes everything you could need.

> **MCAT STRATEGY > > >**
>
> Don't delay! Sign up for your free online MCAT prep bundle today.

If you don't have the time, inclination, or budget to sign up for a course, you can pull together the self-study resources you need to cover content, practice, and simulated Full Length practice MCATs. The best combination here is the full set of Next Step MCAT books, the AAMC online prep bundle, and the 10-pack of Next Step full length exams. Combining those three resources will provide you with thousands of questions, hundreds of practice passages, and over a dozen full exams.

After signing up for a course, or purchasing the self-study resources you need, it's time to make the best possible use of those resources. It all begins with setting up a study plan.

1. Set a Study Schedule

There are three ways to set up a study schedule: work backwards from Test Day, forwards from the current date, or simply use the online Next Step study plan generator.

The last option is by far the simplest and easiest. As a part of the free online Next Step prep bundle, you will have access to the study plan generator. This is a tool that is exclusive to Next Step—a study plan that asks you a series of simple questions and then generates a day-by-day plan that is personalized to your calendar.

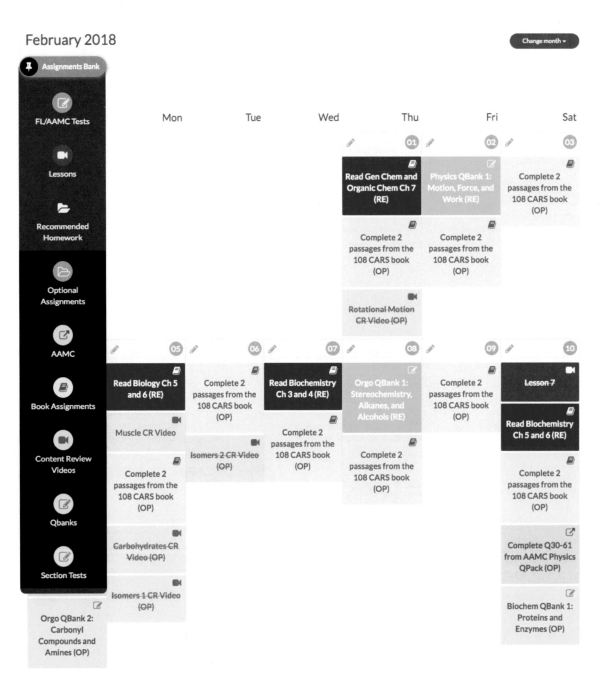

Figure 1. An example of the day-by-day checklist provided by the Next Step study plan generator.

If you prefer to make your study plan by hand, you can either work forward from the first day of prep, or work backwards from Test Day. Neither is necessarily a superior choice, it simply depends on whether or not you've already registered for the exam. Here's an example of a basic algorithm you might use working backwards from Test Day:

1. Start with your calendar of commitments. When are you traveling for work? Taking final exams? Celebrating holidays or taking care of other commitments? Block those days out.

2. Next, working backwards from Test Day, assign yourself Full Length exams. Which day of the week is best for you? When can you commit to taking an entire seven hour test? Typically you want to space the tests out roughly once every 4-9 days.

3. Assign the day after a Full Length as a test review day. Yes, it'll take the whole day.

4. Next, assign yourself the Next Step MCAT Diagnostic test on the first day of prep.

5. Then plan out how you will complete your content review. If using the Next Step review books, simply assign chapters at a pace you can keep up with—anything from one every other day up to five or more a day can be reasonable based on your own learning speed and other commitment.

6. Build in content review days and the occasional day off.

7. Once you've got your content review assigned and your Full Length exams allocated, fill the remainder of the schedule with additional practice—passages from the Next Step 108 Verbal book, for example, or questions from the online QBank that comes with the Next Step 10-pack of online Full Lengths.

After making the schedule, stick to it! Keep up with the assignments you've given yourself. To get the most out of your schedule, you'll want to use two important tools: a Lessons Learned Journal and a good Study Group.

MCAT STRATEGY > > >

Give yourself days off! Burnout is a real thing and if you don't plan in some catch up days or days off, you'll rapidly fall behind. The further you fall behind, the more discouraged you can get. Prevent this problem from ever coming up by giving yourself mental health breaks throughout your plan.

2. Lessons Learned Journal

Every time you do a practice passage or set of independent questions, you should be reviewing them thoroughly—both the ones you got right and the ones you got wrong. Ultimately, while prepping it doesn't matter if you get questions right or wrong. Your score on practice tests doesn't matter. The *only* thing that matters is *what you learn for Test Day*. Since the only score that counts is the one you get on the real MCAT, all of your prep should be future-oriented. The question you ask yourself is not "why did I get this question wrong?" but rather "what does getting this question wrong in the manner that I got it wrong teach me about Test Day, and how do I get it right on the real exam?"

If you would like to see an in-depth discussion of how to craft a Lessons Learned journal, and see some examples of what a Lessons Learned journal looks like, watch the free Lesson 1 under the "Lesson Videos" tab of your online free MCAT prep bundle at nextstepmcat.com.

3. Study Groups

The best way to prep for the MCAT is free. That bears repeating: the single best way to prep for the MCAT is free.

Among the biggest challenges to preparing for the MCAT are staying motivated and being able to keep track of how well you are doing. One of the best ways to tackle both of these challenges is a study group. For many, study groups may bring to mind images of harried students huddled around a cramped table, snacks and caffeinated beverages strewn about, toiling away long into the night. However, with the plethora of online meeting platforms and conference-call apps, it is easier than ever to meet with your peers from around the country in the manner or schedule that suits you best.

The exam is a critical part of your application to medical school, and not utilizing a strategy which may help you reach your score goal (due to previous bad experiences) is tempting, but it is not in your best interest. One thing you must remember is that you are not competing against your friends, classmates, or study group members on the test. This line of thinking is highly misguided, as tens of thousands of students sit for the MCAT each year and, as the AAMC has repeatedly stated, there is no "curve" to the exam. If someone tells you a study group is bad because it takes away an advantage you may have by keeping "Test Day secrets" to yourself, ignore them.

There are complications with study groups of course. For example, the new Psych/Soc section of the exam should have you familiar with the concept of social loafing. You will have people who may not pull their weight in the group, or who serve as a distraction. If that happens, tell them the problem and if necessary, let them go and move on. In an online study group, this process is relatively painless. There will be differing levels of dedication among group members, and if you are not diligent, study sessions can devolve into socializing, or watching videos online. Group turnover may be high if you do not coordinate test dates, as people may not stick with the group long enough to get the desired results or to justify the time it took to form the group in the first place. The efficacy of your group depends prominently on the study habits of people that you can pull in. Do your vetting, or find a group which has already formed and worked. One of the most successful study groups formed via the Next Step forums (http://forum.nextstepmcat.com) has been going on for over a year, with new students filtering in and older students filtering out as they sit for their official test. This can eliminate much of the up-font cost of starting a study group.

MCAT STRATEGY > > >

A study group provides social support as well as academic support. It's like joining a gym as opposed to trying to just workout at home with equipment. The peer pressure of being around other MCAT preppers can be harnessed to positive effect—it will keep you moving on the MCAT treadmill!

If chosen properly, the pros of an MCAT study group vastly outweigh the cons. The flipside of social loafing is social facilitation, since being in a group can force you to really test yourself by explaining a concept to another member (in medicine, the concept of "see one, do one, teach one" is a standard for assessing mastery). Groups allow you to learn much more than you could on your own, as you can each break down a part of the test, or take the study materials and split them up. Careful member selection allows group members to take advantage of one another's strengths. Using online surveys or forms for new members can allow you to best match the study group needs with member strengths and weaknesses. As students have found using the Next Step forums, a group will allow you to draw on collective resources, such as study guides, mnemonics, and content or strategy resources.

The single best reason to try out a study group stems from the truth that no matter who you are, what your major is/was, or how well you have done in school, the real task of the MCAT is learning to think the way the test makers want us to. Unless you spend years with the exam as the Next Step faculty has, the AAMC does not offer much insight into their way of thinking. In the 3-4 months most students spend on their prep it can be almost impossible to develop this insight on your own. Modifying your way of thinking to fit the test can be difficult, especially if you have always been successful doing things your way. Working with others offers the best chance to learn to see the MCAT passages and questions in different ways. Keeping this in mind, and following the advice above to avoid potential problems, an online or in-person study group can be a motivating, fun, and productive part of your journey towards medical school.

4. Must-Knows

> The MCAT asks a lot of us. Rising to the challenge means staying organized. First things first: make a study schedule!
> – The simplest way to do this is using the free study schedule tool available as a part of the free Next Step MCAT prep bundle: https://nextsteptestprep.com/mcat-resources-page/
> It's not about getting questions right or wrong, it's about learning from your successes and mistakes to improve your performance on Test Day. Start a journal and keep track of all of your Lessons Learned.
> Get help! Study groups are used in every single medical school (sometimes as a required part of the curriculum) and you should use them in your MCAT prep.
> – The Next Step forums include several threads dedicated to helping students find study groups and study buddies: http://forum.nextstepmcat.com/

6

This page left intentionally blank.

How to Study MCAT Science

CHAPTER 2

0. Introduction

The amount of content the MCAT expects you to know can seem staggering. But don't despair! By keeping a few simple principles in mind, you can master all of the needed science content. To make sure you learn the science in a way that sticks, practice spaced repetition, active engagement, and use varied modalities of learning.

1. Spaced Repetition

Every time you learn something, you start forgetting it almost immediately. Each time you re-learn it, however, the forgetting happens more slowly. After re-learning something for a third or fourth time, it can really stick. Most importantly, it'll stick through Test Day.

> **MCAT STRATEGY > > >**
>
> The MCAT asks a lot of us. But you can do it!

The process of repeating content after certain intervals of time is called spaced repetition. You repeat the content, spaced out over time. Our brains need rest and sleep to really consolidate memories, so for the MCAT we should follow what is called the Rule of 2's: repeat information after two hours and then again after two days. Finally, do a day of full content review after two weeks.

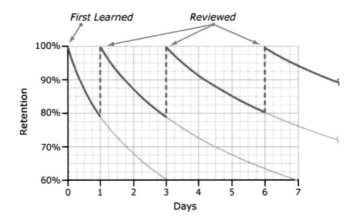

Figure 2. The curve of forgetting.

It can be tempting to always want to plow ahead—after all the MCAT always has new information we need to learn. By constantly moving forward without giving your brain time to properly master material simply guarantees that it will all be forgotten by Test Day.

2. Active Engagement

One of the most common mistakes Next Step tutors see their students make is being too passive. Students think that because they're taking notes while listening to a lecture, they're learning. Or that by reading and re-reading and re-re-reading the same set of notes, they're developing a mastery of the material.

While *some* learning is certainly taking place, it's not the *best* way to learn. The real MCAT is going to be an experience defined by answering questions, not just passively jotting down notes. So your prep needs to take the same sort of active engagement process to learning.

Two tools that help with active engagement are ***taking questions instead of notes*** and making ***study sheets***. "Taking questions" means that when listening to a lecture (something like a Khan Academy video or a Next Step content review video), you periodically pause the video and jot down a question. You don't write down what the lecturer just said, you write down a question for which the lecture is the answer.

That is, say you're watching a lecture on amino acids, and the video says "we should remember that proline is unique because it is the only amino acid whose side chain connects to its own amino backbone." Instead of jotting down "Pro unique b/c connect own amino grp" you would write down "Proline unique because: _____"

Then, two hours later you would come back and see if you can answer the questions you jotted down from the lecture. If you can't remember any of them, re-watch the video. Two days later, return to your questions and answer them again. Finally, two weeks later when you're doing a content review day, answer the questions you took from all of the lectures or chapters you've done over the past two weeks.

Next, you should get in the habit of making study sheets. A study sheet in a single sheet of paper on which you summarize a particular topic (say a chart of all 20 amino acids). You then copy the sheet and blank out some information and quiz yourself—can you fill in the missing information? The next day, blank out more information and quiz yourself again. Repeat this process until you're staring a blank sheet of paper with a title at the top, and see if you can, purely from memory, recreate the entire study sheet. Here's an example of a study sheet that's a table of all the hormones you have to memorize for the MCAT:

Hormone	Secreted by	In response to	Effect	Type
Oxytocin	Posterior Pituitary	Childbirth	Uterine contraction, Emotional Bonding	Peptide
Vasopressin (ADH)	Posterior Pituitary	High plasma osmolality	Retain water, ↑ aquaporin channels in collecting duct, DCT	Peptide
FSH	Anterior Pituitary	GnRH	♀: initiate follicle growth ♂: ↑ spermatocyte development ♀, ♂: maturation of germ cells	Glycoprotein
LH	Anterior Pituitary	GnRH ♀: estrogen spike from follicle just before ovulation	♀: ovulation, follicle becomes corpus luteum ♂: Leydig cells → ↑testosterone	Glycoprotein
ACTH	Anterior Pituitary	CRH, Stress	↑ adrenal release of corticosteroids	Peptide
TSH	Anterior Pituitary	TRH, low plasma levels of T_4 and T_3	↑ thyroid release of T_4 and T_3	Glycoprotein
Prolactin	Anterior Pituitary	Falling progesterone at end of pregnancy	Mammary gland enlargement, milk production	Peptide
Endorphin	Anterior Pituitary	Pain	Pain relief	Peptide
Growth Hormone	Anterior Pituitary	GHRH	Growth of long bones, general anabolism	Peptide
Calcitonin	Thyroid	High plasma $[Ca^{2+}]$	Reduce plasma $[Ca^{2+}]$	Peptide
T_4 & T_3	Thyroid	TSH	↑ metabolic rate	Amino Acid Tyr, but act like steroid
Parathyroid Horm.	Parathyroid	Low plasma $[Ca^{2+}]$	↑ plasma $[Ca^{2+}]$	Peptide
Glucagon	Pancreas α cells	Low blood [Glucose]	↑ blood [Glucose]	Peptide
Insulin	Pancreas β cells	High blood [Glucose]	↓ blood [Glucose]	Peptide
Somatostatin	Pancreas δ cells	Various, usually high hormone levels	Suppress: GH, TSH, CCK, insulin, glucagon	Peptide
Cortisol	Adrenal Cortex	Stress	↑ [Glucose], Immune suppression	Steroid
Aldosterone	Adrenal Cortex	ACTH, ATII, low bp	Collecting Duct, DCT: reabsorb Na^+, Secrete K^+, water retention, ↑ bp	Steroid
Epinephrine	Adrenal Medulla	Sudden stress	Sympathetic response: ↑ heart rate, breathing, etc.	Peptide / Tyr derivative
Estrogen	♀: Ovaries, ♂: Adrenal	FSH	♀: secondary sex characteristics, endometrial development during menstrual cycle, surge leads to LH surge	Steroid
Progestrone	♀: Ovary: Corpus Luteum, ♂: Adrenal	Ovulation	Thicken, maintain endometrium in preparation for implantation	Steroid
Testosterone	♂: Leydig cells of testes, ♀: Ovaries	GnRH→LH→Testos.	Development, maintenance of secondary sex characteristics	Steroid
Norepinephrine	Adrenal Medulla	Sudden stress	Sympath. responses of fight or flight	Peptide / Tyr derivative
hCG	Placenta	Implantation	Maintains corpus luteum at start of pregnancy	Glycoprotein
GnRH	Hypothalamus	Puberty, Menses	↑ LH, FSH release	Peptide

Figure 3. A sample study sheet.

Hormone	Secreted by	In response to	Effect	Type
Oxytocin		Childbirth	Uterine contraction, Emotional Bonding	Peptide
Vasopressin (ADH)	Posterior Pituitary	High plasma osmolality	Retain water, ↑ aquaporin channels in collecting duct, DCT	
	Anterior Pituitary	GnRH	♀: initiate follicle growth ♂: ↑ spermatocyte development ♀, ♂: maturation of germ cells	Glycoprotein
LH	Anterior Pituitary	GnRH ♀: estrogen spike from follicle just before ovulation		Glycoprotein
ACTH	Anterior Pituitary		↑ adrenal release of corticosteroids	Peptide
TSH	Anterior Pituitary	TRH, low plasma levels of T_4 and T_3	↑ thyroid release of T_4 and T_3	
	Anterior Pituitary	Falling progesterone at end of pregnancy	Mammary gland enlargement, milk production	Peptide
Endorphin	Anterior Pituitary		Pain relief	Peptide
Growth Hormone		GHRH	Growth of long bones, general anabolism	Peptide
Calcitonin	Thyroid	High plasma $[Ca^{2+}]$		Peptide
T_4 & T_3	Thyroid		↑ metabolic rate	Amino Acid Tyr, but act like steroid
Parathyroid Horm.	Parathyroid	Low plasma $[Ca^{2+}]$	↑ plasma $[Ca^{2+}]$	
Glucagon		Low blood [Glucose]	↑ blood [Glucose]	Peptide
Insulin	Pancreas β cells	High blood [Glucose]	↓ blood [Glucose]	Peptide
Somatostatin	Pancreas δ cells		Suppress: GH, TSH, CCK, insulin, glucagon	Peptide
	Adrenal Cortex	Stress	↑ [Glucose], Immune suppression	Steroid
Aldosterone	Adrenal Cortex		Collecting Duct, DCT: reabsorb Na^+, Secrete K^+, water retention, ↑ bp	Steroid
Epinephrine	Adrenal Medulla	Sudden stress	Sympathetic response: ↑ heart rate, breathing, etc.	
Estrogen	♀: Ovaries, ♂: Adrenal		♀: secondary sex characteristics, endometrial development during menstrual cycle, surge leads to LH surge	Steroid
Progesterone		Ovulation	Thicken, maintain endometrium in preparation for implantation	Steroid
	♂: Leydig cells of testes, ♀: Ovaries	GnRH→LH→Testos.	Development, maintenance of secondary sex characteristics	Steroid
Norepinephrine	Adrenal Medulla	Sudden stress		Peptide / Tyr derivative
hCG		Implantation	Maintains corpus luteum at start of pregnancy	Glycoprotein
GnRH	Hypothalamus		↑ LH, FSH release	Peptide

Hormone	Secreted by	In response to	Effect	Type
Oxytocin		Childbirth	Uterine contraction, Emotional Bonding	
Vasopressin (ADH)		High plasma osmolality	Retain water, ↑ aquaporin channels in collecting duct, DCT	
		GnRH	♀: initiate follicle growth ♂: ↑ spermatocyte development ♀, ♂: maturation of germ cells	
LH		GnRH ♀: estrogen spike from follicle just before ovulation		
ACTH			↑ adrenal release of corticosteroids	
TSH		TRH, low plasma levels of T_4 and T_3		
		Falling progesterone at end of pregnancy	Mammary gland enlargement, milk production	
Endorphin			Pain relief	
Growth Hormone		GHRH	Growth of long bones, general anabolism	
Calcitonin		High plasma $[Ca^{2+}]$		
T_4 & T_3			↑ metabolic rate	
Parathyroid Horm.		Low plasma $[Ca^{2+}]$	↑ plasma $[Ca^{2+}]$	
Glucagon		Low blood [Glucose]	↑ blood [Glucose]	
Insulin		High blood [Glucose]	↓ blood [Glucose]	
Somatostatin			Supress: GH, TSH, CCK, insulin, glucagon	
		Stress	↑ [Glucose], Immune suppression	
Aldosterone			Collecting Duct, DCT: reabsorb Na^+, Secrete K^+, water retention, ↑ bp	
Epinephrine			Sympathetic response: ↑ heart rate, breathing, etc.	
Estrogen			♀: secondary sex characteristics, endometrial development during menstrual cycle, surge leads to LH surge	
Progestrone		Ovulation	Thicken, maintain endometrium in preparation for implantation	
		GnRH→LH→Testos.	Development, maintenance of secondary sex characteristics	
Norepinephrine		Sudden stress		
hCG			Maintains corpus luteum at start of pregnancy	
GnRH			↑ LH, FSH release	

Hormone	Secreted by	In response to	Effect	Type
Oxytocin				
Vasopressin (ADH)				
FSH				
LH				
ACTH				
TSH				
Prolactin				
Endorphin				
Growth Hormone				
Calcitonin				
T_4 & T_3				
Parathyroid Horm.				
Glucagon				
Insulin				
Somatostatin				
Cortisol				
Aldosterone				
Epinephrine				
Estrogen				
Progestrone				
Testosterone				
Norepinephrine				
hCG				
GnRH				

3. Varied Modalities

Different people learn differently. There's no single "best" method to learn MCAT science, there's only *your* best method. Are you visual learner? An auditory one? A kinesthetic learner? However you learn best, you should try to engage with the material in multiple different modalities.

An example of how this might work is by developing mnemonics that connect with your personal style of learning. Let's say you want to learn the list of which gases are diatomic under standard conditions. If you're a visual learner, you might memorize it as an L-shape on the periodic table:

1 **H** **1.008**																	**2** He 4.00
3 Li 6.94	4 Be 9.01											5 B 10.81	6 C 12.01	**7** **N** **14.01**	**8** **O** **16.00**	**9** **F** **19.00**	10 Ne 20.18
11 Na 22.99	12 Mg 24.31											13 Al 26.98	14 Si 28.09	15 P 30.97	16 S 32.07	**17** **Cl** **35.45**	18 Ar 39.95
19 K 39.10	20 Ca 40.08	21 Sc 44.96	22 Ti 47.88	23 V 50.94	24 Cr 52.00	25 Mn 54.94	26 Fe 55.85	27 Co 58.93	28 Ni 58.69	29 Cu 63.55	30 Zn 65.39	31 Ga 69.72	32 Ge 72.61	33 As 74.92	34 Se 76.96	**35** **Br** **79.90**	36 Kr 83.80
37 Rb 85.47	38 Sr 87.62	39 Y 88.91	40 Zr 91.22	41 Nb 92.91	42 Mo 95.94	43 Tc (98)	44 Ru 101.1	45 Rh 102.9	46 Pd 106.4	47 Ag 107.9	48 Cd 112.4	49 In 114.8	50 Sn 118.71	51 Sb 121.75	52 Te 127.60	**53** **I** **126.90**	54 Xe 131.29

Figure 4. A visual mnemonic.

Alternatively, if you're an auditory learner, you might make a mnemonic that has a good auditory rhythm to it: **h**ave **n**o **f**ear **of i**ce **c**old **b**eer, which reminds us the gases are H_2, N_2, F_2, O_2, I_2, Cl_2, Br_2.

Learning things kinesthetically means tying them to movement, to your body, or to spatial relationships. An obvious example here is the right hand rule for determining the interactions between a magnetic field and a moving charge.

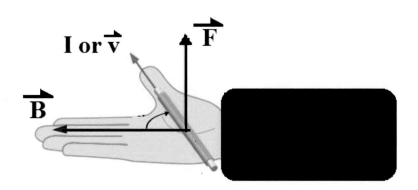

Figure 5. The right hand rule.

When memorizing the right hand rule, you can remember that you have many fingers and magnetic fields are drawn with many lines (or alternatively, "f-f for fingers-field"). Your thumb is held out like a hitchhiker—it represents movement (of charge or current) just like sticking a thumb out meant you wanted to move in a particular direction when hitchhiking. Finally your palm represents the push (or force) of the magnetic field. So while holding your hand up in front of you, you can recite to yourself "fingers field, palm push, thumb hitchhikes along" and you've created a mnemonic that's grounded in the physical reality of your hand, helping those with kinesthetic learning styles.

4. Must-Knows

> Your brain won't truly learn something unless you repeat the information and sleep between repetitions.
> – Review your content using the Rule of 2: repeat after 2 hours, 2 days, and 2 weeks.
> You're not training to be a scribe, you're training to be a doctor! Stop just writing notes down or passively reading/watching science content. Engage actively!
> – Don't take notes, take **questions**. Create study sheets, flashcards, and other exercises that require you to active respond to information.
> Variety is the spice of life. Engage with the material in a way that's auditory, kinesthetic, and visual. Pace around your room and gesture. Talk out loud to yourself. Draw out goofy cartoons or other simple diagrams. Activate your whole brain!

Active Reading Techniques

0. Introduction

Some people will try to tell you that there's a single "best" way to do the CARS section of the MCAT. Needless to say, that's wrong. There are as many different right approaches as there are test-takers. After all, everyone's brain works a little differently. So the first thing you want to do is to find an approach that makes the most sense *for you*.

To that end, we're going to discuss three different approaches to the passages. You should start by practicing these approaches to find one that suits you best. Then, start to make adjustments as needed as you practice more.

1. Time and Tools

To begin with, let's discuss two major factors: the tools at your disposal and how to allocate time.

First, on Test Day you have two simple tools to deal with the CARS passages: ***your marker*** and wet-erase board, and the ***highlighting function*** on the screen. You're going to need to decide how to use these tools to best effect. Some people like stopping while reading and jotting some notes down. Others like to highlight while they read, but not take any notes. Finally, some people like to just whiz through the passage as quickly as possible without using either the marker or the highlighter.

How should you use these tools?

Marker and wet-erase board: only stop to jot down important ideas. Avoid an overly mechanical approach. Instead, jot down the connections between important ideas as they come up. For some paragraphs, you may write nothing, since there's no important notes. By contrast, other paragraphs may require a bunch of notes.

Highlighter: use this sparingly. If you highlight everything, then you end up highlighting nothing. Don't highlight big chunks of text just "because it looks important". Instead, pick out individual words that capture the author's most important ideas. Highlight key terms, contrasts, opinions, cause-and-effect relationships.

Key terms: Any proper nouns that look important. Names, dates, other technical terms that you want to be able to find again quickly. For example, Isaac Newton, post-1989, categorical imperative, CDC.

Opinion: Most importantly, the author's opinion. This can mean the opinion of a person, or of an entire school of thought. For example, "Postmodernism fundamentally rejects a static, universal view of science" is just as much an opinion as, "Picasso found his early work to be too constrained and 'adult-looking'."

Contrast: Any contrasts that show up between people, ideas, cultures, etc. For example: old vs. new, author vs. art critic, French vs. Vietnamese, radical vs. conservative

Cause and effect: For the purposes of this book, we are using the term "cause and effect" in a very loose, rhetorical sense. We're referring to any connections between ideas that have a because-therefore relationship. For example, "The existence of a successful democracy depends upon high quality free public education," "The initial step in the formation of a dental cavity is adherence of the lactic-acid secreting bacteria to the enamel of the tooth, following by plaque deposition," and "Rising income levels have a direct correlation with civic engagement as measured by voting behavior."

How should you allocate your time?

You will have 10 minutes to read a passage, analyze its content, and answer all of the questions that go with it. Broadly speaking, you can spend that time in three ways: mainly on the questions, mainly on the passage, or split evenly between them.

The most common approach, and the one that is most successful for more students is an even-split approach. Spend about 4.5 minutes reading the passage, and then 5.5 minutes answering the questions. This way you have enough time to carefully consider the ideas presented in the text, while still having enough time to occasionally go back and look up materials to help you answer the questions.

However, some students find that they're not ever comfortable answering a question unless they go back and look something up in the passage. For those students, they should move quickly through the passage (only 1.5 minutes) and then spend the bulk of their time very carefully analyzing each question and looking for support in the passage.

Finally, a student with an exceptional short-term memory may find it better to slow down on the passage, read each sentence and paragraph two (or even three) times in order to really "master" the passage over the course of six or seven minutes. That only leaves a few minutes to move very quickly through the questions.

2. Three approaches to the passage

Now that we've looked at the different tools you have available and seen three possible ways to spend your time on the test, let's discuss the three possible approaches to the passages.

Approach I: The Highlighting Technique

This balanced technique is by far the most popular, most common, and most successful.

Passage: 4.5 minutes

Highlighter: Key terms, contrast, opinion, cause-and-effect

Wet-erase board: don't use

Question: 5.5 minutes

With this approach, you will be using the highlighter as your main tool for synthesizing what you're reading. You must ***absolutely NOT highlight as you go along***. Instead, stop every 3-4 sentences, ask yourself, "okay what did I just read?" and then select a few words that capture the important ideas you just read. If you just highlight as you read along, you end up with the "paint roller effect" where everything gets highlighted.

Then, when you get to the end of the passage take a moment to ask yourself what the Main Idea was of what you've just read. Focus on the author's overall opinion and tone. You needn't write it down, but some students find it helpful to do so.

When solving questions, you should be aiming to answer 2-3 of them without looking anything up, and then 2-3 of them may require you to go back and look up facts from the passage. Since you'll have something like 5 minutes to answer the questions, you should have plenty of time do to a bit of "look it up" work.

On the next page you'll find two practice passages. Get a highlighter pen and work through them—don't worry about time for now. Focus on making good choices about what to highlight. Then answer the questions.

After that, you'll see our explanations. There, we have done some sample highlighting of the text as a way to indicate what's worth highlighting. Compare your choices to our suggestions to see if you missed anything important, or highlighted something that was a minor detail.

Compare your highlighting choices to what came up in the questions—did your highlighting help focus your attention on the things that came up in the questions? If so, great job! If not, you can help your review by going back through the passage with another color of highlighter pen and "fixing" the highlighting so that it's perfect. Then come back and review the passage a week later to remind yourself about what good highlighting looks like.

Highlighting Practice Passage I

Epiphenomenalism is a theory of mind that posits that mental events are caused by underlying physical events, but that those mental events cannot then cause physical changes. That is, it is not the subjective sensation of nervousness that causes perspiration, but rather the perspiration is caused by a physiological reaction. This reaction also produces a sensation of nervousness, but that "feeling" is just a side-effect. Thomas Henry Huxley likened the mind to the whistle on a steam locomotive; while the whistle may announce that the train is coming, it has no effect on the actual operation of the train itself.

The development of epiphenomenalism as a school of thought is rooted in the attempt to solve the basic problem of Cartesian dualism. In the 19th century, philosophers wrestled with the problem of interaction between two seemingly incompatible substances: the mental and the physical. The huge successes of the Enlightenment and the scientific tradition that grew out of it demonstrated humanity's increasing mastery over the realm of the physical, but the mental remained largely opaque, governed by theories and attitudes that could at best be called "folk psychology". In light of this disparity, thinkers in the early 19th century wondered how it was that mind and body could interact.

Descartes posited that there was a special organ—the pineal gland—in the center of the brain that provided a two-way link between the substances of mind and body. This organ explained the truth of our basic perception that the body can affect the mind (e.g. putting wine into the body can cloud the mind), and that the mind can affect the body (e.g. our desire to get some fresh air can send the body out for a walk).

The epiphenomenalists countered that although the mind may be a substance different from the body, it has no causative power on the body. This view flourished as it was consonant with the scientific behaviorism that was coming into vogue at the turn of the 20th century. Such scientific behaviorists, notably Ivan Pavlov, John Watson, and Burrhus Skinner, found great success in their efforts to investigate the relationship between environmental stimuli and behavior exhibited by animals (including humans), while making no reference whatsoever to the mental state of the subject. While such behaviorists would not have made the absurd proposal that the subject has no mental state at all, they simply treated the mental state as causally irrelevant. If an animal's "feelings" cannot have any effect on its behavior, then we may safely ignore them in constructing our experiments and our theories about how animals behave, they held.

Epiphenomenalism faced a number of challenges throughout the past century, but since the cognitive revolution in the 1960's, it has received a number of surprising new avenues of support. In the more modern understanding, mental states are simply physical states in the brain–a thought is simply a pattern of electrical impulses traveling along neurons, a memory a growth of new connections between neurons, a feeling an increased level of certain neurotransmitters in certain anatomical regions. The epiphenomenon is the purely subjective, qualitative aspect of an experience. Such aspects are usually referred to as the "raw feel" of an experience, or the "what-it-is-like", or most often, "qualia". Thus if a dog and a robot that can perfectly mimic the behavior of a dog are both fed a piece of bacon, they will exhibit exactly the same behavior, but only the real dog will be experiencing the qualia of the food. The saltiness of the salt, the richness of the smell, the pleasure of eating will only be present in the epiphenomenal world that is the dog's brain. Both will bark happily, wag their tails, and scarf the food down in a single bite, but only the dog has a mind that will be experiencing the qualia of the food.

A large body of neurophysiological data seem to support epiphenomenalism. Such data includes a number of kinds of electrical potentials which occur in the brain and which cause behavior, and yet happen before the subject is mentally aware of the event. Research shows that it takes at least half a second for a stimulus to become part of conscious experience, and yet subjects are capable of reacting to that stimulus in less than half that time. Thus it is not our consciousness that controls our behavior, but rather our brain reacts and the "mental feeling" of what's happening comes after the fact.

1. Consider the case of the dog and dog-like robot discussed in the fifth paragraph. Descartes would assert that:
   A. the existence of a robot dog that can perfectly mimic the real dog refutes his theory of dualism.
   B. both the real dog and the robot dog have minds that are linked to their bodies through the pineal gland.
   C. the real dog has a rudimentary mind that is fundamentally different from its body, whereas the robot has only a body.
   D. the robot dog's qualia have some additional, unknowable property that separates the robot dog from the real one.

2. According to the passage, the raw feel of an experience arises from a brain state that is also the cause of any behavior we exhibit in response to that experience but that the feel itself is causally irrelevant. That view would most be *weakened* if it were discovered that which of the following were true?
   A. The electrical potentials that happen in response to a stimulus before the subject is aware of the experience happen most strikingly in the case of olfactory stimuli.
   B. When a subject is unconscious they are still capable of reacting to a number of different stimuli.
   C. Anger management classes have been shown to stimulate a portion of the prefrontal cortex that is associated with "cooling down" and "thinking things through before you act" and that those regions exhibit activity before subsequent behavioral actions designed to reduce physiological arousal.
   D. Meditation techniques that teach a person to avoid harmful repetitive thought patterns have been shown to be effective in the treatment of a number of mental illnesses that had previously only been considered treatable through powerful drugs or surgery.

3. Why does the author discuss the belief of Descartes that the brain has a special gland to mediate interactions between the body and the soul?
   A. To show that Descartes's error about the function of the pineal gland serves as a fatal blow to the soundness of his philosophical theory.
   B. To refute Descartes's theory of mind/body dualism.
   C. To acknowledge that even Descartes knew that true dualism was impossible and that the mind must, at least in part, be a physical thing.
   D. To demonstrate that Descartes was aware that physical things that affect the body could alter the mind even though the mind is a fundamentally different substance from the body.

4. The common experience of a violent shocked reaction (shouting, flinching, etc.) when seeing someone in the same room when you thought you were alone, even when that person is someone very familiar serves as evidence:
   A. for both epiphenomenalism and materialism.
   B. for neither dualism nor epiphenomenalism.
   C. for dualism but not epiphenomenalism.
   D. against the notion that mind/body interactions are mediated by the pineal gland.

5. Which of the following is most analogous to the function of the mind in epiphenomenalism?
   A. The gasoline used to run a motor that drives a boat forward.
   B. The beauty of a flower that inspires a poet to write a poem.
   C. The tension an audience feels while watching a suspenseful movie.
   D. The sunlight glinting off waves on the surface of a calm lake.

6. In an experiment subjects are made to look at a series of shocking and disturbing images flashed on the screen for a very short period of time. What does the passage suggest may happen in the brains of these subjects?
   A. Their pineal glands will suffer stress in response to the disturbing images.
   B. Some physiological responses may occur before the subject is mentally aware of what they're looking at.
   C. The parts of their brains responsible for registering disgust will be stimulated only after the subjects have a subjective feeling of disgust.
   D. At least some of the subjects will stop looking at the screen after they realize the images are all disturbing.

Highlighting Practice Passage I

Epiphenomenalism is a theory of mind that posits that mental events are caused by underlying physical events, but that those mental events cannot then cause physical changes. That is, it is not the subjective sensation of nervousness that causes perspiration, but rather the perspiration is caused by a physiological reaction. This reaction also produces a sensation of nervousness, but that "feeling" is just a side-effect. Thomas Henry Huxley likened the mind to the whistle on a steam locomotive; while the whistle may announce that the train is coming, it has no effect on the actual operation of the train itself.

Here we've highlighted two technical words—epiphenomenalism and Huxley's name. That's so we can find them again later. We've also highlighted some terms that reveal opinion—the opinion of epiphenomenalism. Remember that opinions can be a school of thought.

The development of epiphenomenalism as a school of thought is rooted in the attempt to solve the basic problem of Cartesian dualism. In the 19th century, philosophers wrestled with the problem of interaction between two seemingly incompatible substances: the mental and the physical. The huge successes of the Enlightenment and the scientific tradition that grew out of it demonstrated humanity's increasing mastery over the realm of the physical, but the mental remained largely opaque, governed by theories and attitudes that could at best be called "folk psychology". In light of this disparity, thinkers in the early 19th century wondered how it was that mind and body could interact.

We're given another opinion here—the opinion of philosophers. Highlighting "interaction" "seemingly incompatible" lets us know what they were thinking, "how it was that mind and body could interact".

Descartes posited that there was a special organ—the pineal gland—in the center of the brain that provided a two-way link between the substances of mind and body. This organ explained the truth of our basic perception that the body can affect the mind (e.g. putting wine into the body can cloud the mind), and that the mind can affect the body (e.g. our desire to get some fresh air can send the body out for a walk).

We're told what Descartes thought about the link between mind and body and should highlight appropriately.

The epiphenomenalists countered that although the mind may be a substance different from the body, it has no causative power on the body. This view flourished as it was consonant with the scientific behaviorism that was coming into vogue at the turn of the 20th century. Such scientific behaviorists, notably Ivan Pavlov, John Watson, and Burrhus Skinner, found great success in their efforts to investigate the relationship between environmental stimuli and behavior exhibited by animals (including humans), while making no reference whatsoever to the mental state of the subject. While such behaviorists would not have made the absurd proposal that the subject has no mental state at all, they simply treated the mental state as causally irrelevant. If an animal's "feelings" cannot have any effect on its behavior, then we may safely ignore them in constructing our experiments and our theories about how animals behave, they held.

Behaviorism supports epiphenomenalism by showing you can analyze and predict behavior with no reference to mental states (not that they don't exist, but they don't matter)

Epiphenomenalism faced a number of challenges throughout the past century, but since the cognitive revolution in the 1960's, it has received a number of surprising new avenues of support. In the more modern understanding, mental states are simply physical states in the brain–a thought is simply a pattern of electrical impulses traveling along neurons, a memory a growth of new connections between neurons, a feeling an increased level of certain neurotransmitters in certain anatomical regions. The epiphenomenon is the purely subjective, qualitative aspect of an experience. Such aspects are usually referred to as the "raw feel" of an experience, or the "what-it-is-like", or most often, "qualia". Thus if a dog and a robot that can perfectly mimic the behavior of a dog are both fed a piece of bacon, they will exhibit exactly the same behavior, but only the real dog will be experiencing the qualia of the food. The saltiness of the salt, the richness of the smell, the pleasure of eating will only be present in the epiphenomenal world that is the dog's brain. Both will bark happily, wag their tails, and scarf the food down in a single bite, but only the dog has a mind that will be experiencing the qualia of the food.

After the cognitive revolution we've come to see mental states as just physical states in the brain. We've given the example of the robot—a robot dog that exactly mimics a real dog could reproduce all of the behaviors but wouldn't experience the qualia the way the dog does.

A large body of neurophysiological data seem to support epiphenomenalism. Such data includes a number of kinds of electrical potentials which occur in the brain and which cause behavior, and yet happen before the subject is mentally aware of the event. Research shows that it takes at least half a second for a stimulus to become part of conscious experience, and yet subjects are capable of reacting to that stimulus in less than half that time. Thus it is not our consciousness that controls our behavior, but rather our brain reacts and the "mental feeling" of what's happening comes after the fact.

The passage wraps up with some new support for epiphenomenalism and we should highlight it.

Main Idea: Epiphenomenalism contrasts with dualism by saying that physical can affect mental but that mental has no control over physical. Support for epiphenomenalism has come from behaviorism, the cognitive revolution, and neurophysiology.

Remember, on Test Day you don't necessarily have to stop and write out the Main Idea. What you do need to do is stop, take a moment to gather your thoughts—look over all of your highlighting, essentially re-skimming the passage just looking to your highlights. In doing so, formulate the Main Idea in your mind.

1. C is correct. Descartes thinks that mind and body are two fundamentally different things, but that they can have a causal relationship with each other through the pineal gland. Descartes would certainly not think that a robot dog had a mind or qualia of any kind.

2. C is correct. To refute epiphenomenalism we need a case where someone can mentally think something through (have a conscious experience of thinking something over) and that thought is able to then cause physical responses. In the case of choice C, the person is able to think things through before activating the physiological response that lets them calm down. Thus C is the correct answer because it suggests that the conscious experience of thinking things through comes before and leads to the actual physiological calming down.

3. D is correct. Descartes believed that mind and body could interact with each other somehow—that mind could cause physical changes and that physical changes (like drinking alcohol) could affect the mind. If mind and body are two very different things, we're left wondering how they could interact. So the author tells us Descartes answer: the brain had a special organ (the pineal gland) to achieve that end.

4. B is correct. The argument about dualism and epiphenomenalism rests on causality: can the mind cause physical changes or not? Dualism says yes, epiphenomenalism says no. Shouting in surprise does not, in itself, address the question. For the situation in the question to be relevant we would have to be told something about the causal links—did the person shout before experiencing surprise, or have the feeling of surprise and then shout in response.

5. D is correct. The example in the passage says that the mind is like the whistle on a train: related to the arrival of the train, but not with any causal power over the train itself. So we need something where the epiphenomenon has no ability to cause the underlying phenomenon. Choice D is the best fit—the glint of sunlight is caused by the small ripples in the water's surface, but the glinting doesn't cause (and can't cause) the underlying waves.

6. B is correct. The final paragraph tells us that some neurophysiology studies have shown that people's brains are capable of reacting faster than the person actually becomes aware of something.

This page left intentionally blank.

Highlighting Practice Passage II

The needs that are usually taken as the starting point for motivation theory are the so-called physiological drives. Two recent lines of research make it necessary to revise our customary notions about these needs, first, the development of the concept of homeostasis, and second, the finding that appetites (preferential choices among foods) are a fairly efficient indication of actual needs or lacks in the body.

[handwritten: motivation theory 2 theories]

Thus it seems impossible as well as useless to make any list of fundamental physiological needs for they can come to almost any number one might wish, depending on the degree of specificity of description. We cannot identify all physiological needs as homeostatic. That sexual desire, sleepiness, sheer activity and maternal behavior in animals, are homeostatic, has not yet been demonstrated. Furthermore, this list would not include the various sensory pleasures (tastes, smells, tickling, stroking) which are probably physiological and which may become the goals of motivated behavior.

[handwritten: not all needs are homeostatic → sensory pleasures]

In a previous paper it has been pointed out that these physiological drives or needs are to be considered unusual rather than typical because they are isolable, and because they are localizable somatically. That is to say, they are relatively independent of each other, of other motivations and of the organism as a whole, and secondly, in many cases, it is possible to demonstrate a localized, underlying somatic base for the drive. This is true less generally than has been thought (exceptions are fatigue, sleepiness, maternal responses) but it is still true in the classic instances of hunger, sex, and thirst.

[handwritten: claim they are isolable so not independent of eachother]

It should be pointed out again that any of the physiological needs and the consummatory behavior involved with them serve as channels for all sorts of other needs as well. That is to say, the person who thinks he is hungry may actually be seeking more for comfort, or dependence, than for vitamins or proteins. Conversely, it is possible to satisfy the hunger need in part by other activities such as drinking water or smoking cigarettes. In other words, relatively isolable as these physiological needs are, they are not completely so.

[handwritten: not isolable → all needs interact w/ eachother]

Undoubtedly these physiological needs are the most pre-potent of all needs. What this means specifically is, that in the human being who is missing everything in life in an extreme fashion, it is most likely that the major motivation would be the physiological needs rather than any others. A person who is lacking food, safety, love, and esteem would most probably hunger for food more strongly than for anything else.

[Adapted from "A Theory of Human Motivation", *Psychological Review*, by A.H. Maslow, 1943.]

1. The author would probably agree with which of the following statements about physiological drives?
    A. A few of the fundamental physiological needs still need to be identified.
    B. Homeostasis is the result of satisfying a physiological need.
    C. The physiological drives do not form a discrete, clearly-defined category.
    D. The strongest physiological drives refer to those needs which are socially-oriented.

2. What is the author's purpose in writing, in the final paragraph, that food would take precedence over the other needs listed?
    A. To support his argument that urgency and priority are a better definition of physiological needs than homeostasis.
    B. To argue that hunger is a fundamental physiological drive, while love and safety aren't.
    C. To show an example of the non-isolable nature of even the fundamental physiological needs.
    D. To prove that fundamental physiological needs cannot be met by alternate activities.

3. An energy-dense drink like soda often meets energy needs far before it provides the person consuming it with a sense of fullness. The passage author would probably consider this:
   A. an example of the overlapping nature of some physiological needs.
   B. evidence of the non-physiological nature of hunger.
   C. evidence that social training can overcome or confuse physiological drives.
   D. an indication that hunger is non-homeostatic.

4. What is the author's purpose in writing, in the second paragraph, that not all physiological needs have been confirmed to be homeostatic?
   A. To support the inclusion of sensory pleasures to the list of recognized physiological needs.
   B. To introduce the unconfirmed needs, sexual desire, sleepiness, maternal instinct, etc.
   C. To provide further evidence against homeostasis as a dominant organizing principle.
   D. To provide evidence that the present definition of physiological needs is problematic.

   └→ present definition is about the homeostasis basis of physiology)

5. Biologist Ernst Mayr argued that complex biological phenomena generally could not always be broken down to sets of simple, isolated relationships, but would remain intertwined and mathematically inexact. The passage author would likely:
   A. agree that biological reductionism is a dead end.
   B. assert that isolability is not, in principle, worth searching for in any phenomena.
   C. acknowledge the difficulty in reductionism, but not its irrelevance.
   D. dismiss the idea that a simple, rule-based understanding can never be achieved.

Highlighting Practice Passage II

The needs that are usually taken as the starting point for motivation theory are the so-called physiological drives. Two recent lines of research make it necessary to revise our customary notions about these needs, first, the development of the concept of homeostasis, and second, the finding that appetites (preferential choices among foods) are a fairly efficient indication of actual needs or lacks in the body.

Thus it seems impossible as well as useless to make any list of fundamental physiological needs for they can come to almost any number one might wish, depending on the degree of specificity of description. We cannot identify all physiological needs as homeostatic. That sexual desire, sleepiness, sheer activity and maternal behavior in animals, are homeostatic, has not yet been demonstrated. Furthermore, this list would not include the various sensory pleasures (tastes, smells, tickling, stroking) which are probably physiological and which may become the goals of motivated behavior.

In a previous paper it has been pointed out that these physiological drives or needs are to be considered unusual rather than typical because they are isolable, and because they are localizable somatically. That is to say, they are relatively independent of each other, of other motivations and of the organism as a whole, and secondly, in many cases, it is possible to demonstrate a localized, underlying somatic base for the drive. This is true less generally than has been thought (exceptions are fatigue, sleepiness, maternal responses) but it is still true in the classic instances of hunger, sex, and thirst.

It should be pointed out again that any of the physiological needs and the consummatory behavior involved with them serve as channels for all sorts of other needs as well. That is to say, the person who thinks he is hungry may actually be seeking more for comfort, or dependence, than for vitamins or proteins. Conversely, it is possible to satisfy the hunger need in part by other activities such as drinking water or smoking cigarettes. In other words, relatively isolable as these physiological needs are, they are not completely so.

Undoubtedly these physiological needs are the most pre-potent of all needs. What this means specifically is, that in the human being who is missing everything in life in an extreme fashion, it is most likely that the major motivation would be the physiological needs rather than any others. A person who is lacking food, safety, love, and esteem would most probably hunger for food more strongly than for anything else.

[Adapted from "A Theory of Human Motivation", *Psychological Review*, by A.H. Maslow, 1943.]

Main Idea: Homeostasis doesn't fully explain even physiological needs as motivators and what may seem like fundamental physiological needs can't fully be isolated, since they may be expressions of emotional needs, or may be satisfied by other behaviors.

1. C is correct. The passage describes the current difficulties in clearly categorizing physiological drives, citing their imperfect isolability as a major issue.
    A. This is not supported by the passage.
    B. This contradicts the passage, which cites several needs that are not homeostatic in nature.
    D. This contradicts the passage, which states that hunger would override drives involving other people, such as love or esteem.

2. **A is correct.** Throughout the passage, the author has been arguing about the difficult in recognizing and categorizing different drives/needs. He shows the problem with homeostasis as a defining factor. In the last paragraph, he returns to some of the currently acknowledged needs, but alights on their pre-potency, demonstrating the urgency to satisfy these needs, and the way they take priority over other needs. The implication is that this definition works where others have failed.

   B. This may be true, but the author seems to have assumed from the start that hunger, one of the classic drives, is physiological. The question at hand was, why is this so?

   C. This paragraph had nothing to do with isolability.

   D. This is contradicted elsewhere in the passage and irrelevant to the section being discussed.

3. **A is correct.** The statement in this question stem suggests that, despite hunger being a drive leading to the ingestion of food, the need can be met, at least from a caloric perspective, without curtailing the hunger itself. This is similar to another example given in the passage, where something with no calories can satisfy hunger, given enough of it, and likewise suggests that needs are not perfectly isolable.

   B. The physiological nature of hunger is not at question in this passage.

   C. Nothing like this is discussed in the passage.

   D. That the hunger drive can be fooled does not necessarily mean it is not homeostatic, and, again, were this evidence, it's not an argument the passage author had made about hunger.

4. **D is correct.** The entire passage is devoted to sussing out the difficulties in identifying the physiological needs, given several contradictory definitions, none of which work for each need traditionally listed. That paragraph is devoted to the issues with the homeostatic definition, but is still in service to that larger goal.

   A. This answer choice switches evidence and conclusion. The sensory pleasures were cited as another problem with the homeostatic definition; the passage author took it as a given that they were physiological in nature.

   B. These were clearly only included as examples to support the claim that many needs are not homeostatic, not the main purpose of the paragraph.

   C. The passage author does not attack homeostasis itself, which explains many bodily processes, merely the definition of physiological needs as homeostatically-motivated.

5. **C is correct.** The passage suggests that the non-isolability of many physiological needs is, in fact, a problem, making it more difficult to understand the drives they feed. At the end, the passage author suggests a new definition, based on a simple hierarchy, to classify physiological and non-physiological needs.

   A. This is not supported by the passage.

   B. Since the passage author explicitly addresses the notion that some phenomena are isolable, it would seem likely that the author thinks its worth searching for isolability.

   D. Too extreme. Reductionism may be desirable, but the passage acknowledges the difficulty.

Approach II: The Note-taking Technique

This slow-read technique is the most common taught in big lecture courses offered by prep companies. It's also one of the least popular among students. The mistake here is that students feel like the note-taking slows them down. They try it once, conclude that they don't like it, and just throw out the whole enterprise.

This is a major mistake—for many students a slow, careful read with judicious note-taking can be very valuable. The key here isn't to write down lots and lots of notes—you wouldn't, for example, write down nearly as many words as you'd highlight when using the highlighting technique.

Instead, the key aspect of the note-taking technique is that you're giving the passage a very thorough, very careful read. The note-taking is simply a way to get you to slow down and focus very precisely on what you're reading. Then, when going through the questions, move fast and never look anything up.

Passage: 6–6.5 minutes
Highlighter: only proper nouns, if any
Wet-erase board: notes after each paragraph
Question: 3.5–4 minutes

Finally, at the end of the passage, ***write down the main idea***. You need to formulate the main idea thoroughly and precisely and get it on paper. Since you're not going to be looking things up in the passage, having the main idea written down on the wet-erase board is a valuable tool.

Ironically, the slow-read approach often works best for students who are very strong readers and are comfortable reading very quickly. Typically students who spent a lot of time reading in college—English majors, philosophy majors, etc.—are the ones that find the most success with this approach.

Because students who are fast readers can move through the sentences very quickly, they can afford to read each sentence or paragraph two (or even three) times to really master what it says.

Again, don't dismiss this approach immediately. Give it plenty of practice to decide if you find it helpful. If, after doing the two practice passages here, the half-section, and the full section that are allocated for note-taking practice, you find you still can't make it work and don't like it, then by all means set this approach aside.

This page left intentionally blank.

Note-taking Practice Passage I

The mere physical vision of the poet may or may not be any keener than the vision of other men. There is an infinite variety in the bodily endowments of habitual verse-makers: there have been near-sighted poets like Tennyson, far-sighted poets like Wordsworth, and, in the well-known case of Robert Browning, a poet conveniently far-sighted in one eye and near-sighted in the other! No doubt the life-long practice of observing and recording natural phenomena sharpens the sense of poets, as it does the senses of Indians, naturalists, sailors and all outdoors men. The quick eye for costume and character possessed by a Chaucer or a Shakespeare is remarkable, but equally so is the observation of a Dickens or a Balzac. It is rather in what we call psychical vision that the poet is wont to excel, that is, in his ability to perceive the meaning of visual phenomena. Here he ceases to be a mere reporter of retinal images, and takes upon himself the higher and harder function of an interpreter of the visible world. He has no immunity from the universal human experiences: he loves and he is angry and he sees men born and die. He becomes according to the measure of his intellectual capacity a thinker. He strives to see into the human heart, to comprehend the working of the human mind. He reads the divine justice in the tragic fall of Kings. He penetrates beneath the external forms of Nature and perceives her as a "living presence." Yet the faculty of vision, which the poet possesses in so eminent a degree, is shared by many who are not poets. Darwin's outward eye was as keen as Wordsworth's; St. Paul's sense of the reality of the invisible world is more wonderful than Shakespeare's. The poet is indeed first of all a seer, but he must be something more than a seer before he is wholly poet. *a good poet not only observes records but feels, and more to be a whole poet*

Another mark of the poetic mind is its vivid sense of relations. The part suggests the whole. In the single instance there is a hint of the general law. The self-same Power that brings the fresh rhodora to the woods brings the poet there also. In the field-mouse, the daisy, the water-fowl, he beholds types and symbols. His own experience stands for all men's. The conscience-stricken Macbeth is a poet when he cries, "Life is a walking shadow," and King Lear makes the same pathetic generalization when he exclaims, "What, have his daughters brought him to this pass?" Through the shifting phenomena of the present the poet feels the sweep of the universe; his mimic play and "the great globe itself" are alike an "insubstantial pageant," though it may happen, as Tennyson said of Wordsworth, that even in the transient he gives the sense of the abiding, "whose dwelling is the light of setting suns." But this perception of relations, characteristic as it is of the poetic temper, is also an attribute of the philosopher. The intellect of a Newton, too, leaps from the specific instance to the general law. *general law for everything not just poets → perceptions*

The real difference between "the poet" and other men is . . . in his capacity for making and employing verbal images of a certain kind, and combining these images into rhythmical and metrical designs. In each of his functions–as "seer," as "maker," and as "singer"–he shows himself a true creator. Criticism no longer attempts to act as his "law-giver," to assert what he may or may not do. The poet is free, like every creative artist, to make a beautiful object in any way he can. And nevertheless criticism–watching countless poets lovingly for many a century, observing their various endowments, their manifest endeavors, their victories and defeats, observing likewise the nature of language, that strange medium (so much stranger than any clay or bronze!) through which poets are compelled to express their conceptions–criticism believes that poetry, like each of the sister arts, has its natural province, its own field of the beautiful. . . . In W. H. Hudson's Green Mansions the reader will remember how a few sticks and stones, laid upon a hilltop, were used as markers to indicate the outlines of a continent. Criticism, likewise, needs its poor sticks and stones of commonplace, if it is to point out any roadway. Our own road leads first into the difficult territory of the poet's imaginings, and then into the more familiar world of the poet's words.

[Adapted from *A Study of Poetry*, Chapter II. Bliss Perry, 1920.]

difference w/ poets
- free
- strange medium
-

1. The passage asserts that the uniqueness of the poet stems from his:
   I. habit of separating himself physically from the drudgery and commonality of day-to-day experience.
   II. acute sense of the immediate as an entity removed from the confounding filter of human interpretation. *immediate?*
   III. ability to reshape verbal imagery according to a specific design.
   A. I only
   B. III only
   C. I and III only
   D. II and III only

2. Throughout the passage, the author advances his primary argument by comparing and contrasting:
   A. the poet and his poetry.
   B. false vision and real experience.
   C. poets and other artists and thinkers.
   D. the subtlety and palpability of poetry.

3. If this passage were included with other pieces of writing on poetry containing central themes consistent with that of this passage, writings with which of the following themes would be most appropriate to include?
   A. Modern native poets
   B. Universal techniques of poetic analysis
   C. That which typifies the poetical → *isolates poetry*
   D. A critical belief that the parallels between poetry and other fine arts threaten the uniqueness of its literary province

4. The sentence "It is rather in what we call psychical vision that the poet is wont to excel, that is, in his ability to perceive the meaning of visual phenomena," in the first paragraph is most probably included by the author in order to:
   A. define the distinct provenance of the poet by offering a descriptive insight into his interpretive process.
   B. highlight the poet's great difficulty in transcending the limitations of immediate vision in their writing.
   C. emphasize the poet's exclusive role as a seer
   D. underscore the uniqueness of the poet's capacity for interpreting the meaning of that which he sees.
   → says that others can do this

5. The author seems to suggest that a reader's appreciation of a poet's work stems from:
   A. the need to separate out the elements of poetry born from the poet's multiple roles as seer, marker and singer.
   B. the difficulty of navigating the literal meaning of a poet's work.
   C. the need to transcend the barrier of dissimilar experience between reader and poet.
   D. the reader finding insight in the mind of a poet.

6. Based upon the passage text, the author most probably finds the role of the critic in relation to the poet to be one of:
   A. imposing strict limitations on the work poets may produce.
   B. interpreting the common elements of poets' work.
   C. liaison, bridging the gap between reader and poet. ← *reader + critic do different things*
   D. judge, putting forth a positive or negative assessment of the absolute merit of poetic works.

7. In the final sentence of the second paragraph, the author makes reference to "The intellect of Newton," in order to:
   A. provide an example illustrating a preceding assertion qualifying an element of the poetic temper.
   B. emphasize his claim that the scientific mind operates differently than that of the poet.
   C. support his assertion that a vivid sense of relation, shared by the philosopher, is necessary and sufficient to define the poetic mind.
   D. strengthen his description of the role of the poet as a thinker according to his "intellectual capacity".

Note-taking Practice Passage I

The mere physical vision of the poet may or may not be any keener than the vision of other men. There is an infinite variety in the bodily endowments of habitual verse-makers: there have been near-sighted poets like Tennyson, far-sighted poets like Wordsworth, and, in the well-known case of Robert Browning, a poet conveniently far-sighted in one eye and near-sighted in the other! No doubt the life-long practice of observing and recording natural phenomena sharpens the sense of poets, as it does the senses of Indians, naturalists, sailors and all outdoors men. The quick eye for costume and character possessed by a Chaucer or a Shakespeare is remarkable, but equally so is the observation of a Dickens or a Balzac. It is rather in what we call psychical vision that the poet is wont to excel, that is, in his ability to perceive the meaning of visual phenomena. Here he ceases to be a mere reporter of retinal images, and takes upon himself the higher and harder function of an interpreter of the visible world. He has no immunity from the universal human experiences: he loves and he is angry and he sees men born and die. He becomes according to the measure of his intellectual capacity a thinker. He strives to see into the human heart, to comprehend the working of the human mind. He reads the divine justice in the tragic fall of Kings. He penetrates beneath the external forms of Nature and perceives her as a "living presence." Yet the faculty of vision, which the poet possesses in so eminent a degree, is shared by many who are not poets. Darwin's outward eye was as keen as Wordsworth's; St. Paul's sense of the reality of the invisible world is more wonderful than Shakespeare's. The poet is indeed first of all a seer, but he must be something more than a seer before he is wholly poet.

Wet-erase Board Notes:

Auth thinks poets are different from other men in their psychical vision, true poet = seer but more than that.

Another mark of the poetic mind is its vivid sense of relations. The part suggests the whole. In the single instance there is a hint of the general law. The self-same Power that brings the fresh rhodora to the woods brings the poet there also. In the field-mouse, the daisy, the water-fowl, he beholds types and symbols. His own experience stands for all men's. The conscience-stricken Macbeth is a poet when he cries, "Life is a walking shadow," and King Lear makes the same pathetic generalization when he exclaims, "What, have his daughters brought him to this pass?" Through the shifting phenomena of the present the poet feels the sweep of the universe; his mimic play and "the great globe itself" are alike an "insubstantial pageant," though it may happen, as Tennyson said of Wordsworth, that even in the transient he gives the sense of the abiding, "whose dwelling is the light of setting suns." But this perception of relations, characteristic as it is of the poetic temper, is also an attribute of the philosopher. The intellect of a Newton, too, leaps from the specific instance to the general law.

Wet-erase Board Notes:

Poet must be seer + able think in univs. + general. Facility for the univs. also in philos + sci

The real difference between "the poet" and other men is . . . in his capacity for making and employing verbal images of a certain kind, and combining these images into rhythmical and metrical designs. In each of his functions–as "seer," as "maker," and as "singer"–he shows himself a true creator. Criticism no longer attempts to act as his "law-giver," to assert what he may or may not do. The poet is free, like every creative artist, to make a beautiful object in any way he can. And nevertheless criticism–watching countless poets lovingly for many a century, observing their various endowments, their manifest endeavors, their victories and defeats, observing likewise the nature of language, that strange medium (so much stranger than any clay or bronze!) through which poets are compelled to express their conceptions–criticism believes that poetry, like each of the sister arts, has its natural province, its own field of the beautiful. . . . In W. H. Hudson's Green Mansions the reader will remember how a few sticks and stones, laid upon a hilltop, were used as markers to indicate the outlines of a continent. Criticism, likewise, needs its poor sticks and stones of commonplace, if it is to point out any roadway. Our own road leads first into the difficult territory of the poet's imaginings, and then into the more familiar world of the poet's words.

[Adapted from *A Study of Poetry*, Chapter II. Bliss Perry, 1920.]

Wet-erase Board Notes:

What sep. poet from other = verbal images in metrical designs, criticism believe poetry beautiful and crit. has own tools to look at poet's imaginings and words.

Main Idea: A poet must have a keen insight into the world, possess an ability to see the universal underlying the particular, and have a unique ability to craft verbal images in a rhythmical pattern. Critics of poetry recognize its beauty and use their own "sticks and stones" to appreciate it.

1. B is correct. I: False. The passage explicitly states in the first paragraph that the poet "has no immunity from the universal human experience."

    II: False. The second paragraph in particular describes the poet's work as having a vivid sense of the relations [between things], of finding a hint of the general in specific instances and, in the second paragraph, as having a "sense of the abiding" and of the "sweep of the universe." Taken together, the author suggests that the poet does not have a strictly isolated sense of the immediate, but that he interprets and relates events by way of his human experience. But, in any case, this statement is incorrect because, from the end of the second paragraph, "this perception of relations, characteristic as it is of the poetic temper, is an also an attribute of the philosopher" and is not, as the question asks, something that is unique to the poet.

    III: True. The passage explains in the last paragraph that "the real difference between "the poet" and other men is . . . in his capacity for making and employing verbal imagery . . . combining these images into rhythmical and metrical designs."

2. C is correct. The main thrust of the passage is describing the common habits of poets and how they are similar or dissimilar to those of other thinkers and artists in support of the passage's main goal of defining what makes a poet unique.

    A. The author never directly compares or contrasts poets with their individual works.

    B. While the passage does explore the nature of a poet's vision, the author explains the process in terms of expanding and interpreting experiences and relationships. He doesn't suggest that any "vision" is less real than "experience."

    D. While the subtlety and palpability of poetry may be referred to obliquely as elements of different poets works in the first and second paragraphs, it's not a continued or central theme of the poet. That main theme is, instead, explaining, as the first sentence of the third paragraph says, "the real difference between 'the poet' and other men."

3. C is correct. The passage seeks out and explains those things that are both common and unique to the poet in the process of writing; such an exposition would fit well in a more general discussion of what defines poetry.

    A. The passage includes examples of poets from different time periods and places, not just modern or native poets. The passage's central theme is what universally makes poets unique from other artists, and doesn't focus on sub-groups of poets.

    B. While the passage does touch on poetic analysis when discussing the place of criticism, it's less central to the passage than the main theme of what uniquely defines poets.

    D. This choice implies that drawing parallels between poetry and other art threatens poetry's place as a separate art form. The third paragraph specifically claims agreement among critics that poetry does occupy its own space in the realm of fine arts contradicting the choice and meaning that any effort to draw parallels between poetry and other art forms would pose no threat to poetry's place.

4. **A is correct.** The sentence gives context to the first paragraph's concluding claim that the poet acts importantly as a seer, by explaining and emphasizing the poet's ability to see psychically (through interpretation in their minds eye) visual phenomena.

   B. This is precisely the opposite of what the sentence claims; according to the sentence, and in keeping with the passage, the poet is adept at transcending the limitations of physical vision and interpreting the implications of both the seen and unseen. Be careful to correctly interpret the use of the word "wont" in the sentence, by keeping in mind the logical progression of the passage.

   C. While the final sentence of the first paragraph does state that the poet must first act as a seer, it continues on to say that ". . . he must be something more than a seer before he is wholly poet." Acting as a seer then, being a "mere reporter of retinal images" as the first paragraph describes it, is a common function performed by many, not by poets exclusively.

   D. This is directly contradicted by the passage's claim that the poet's "faculty of vision . . . is shared by many who are not poets."

5. **D is correct.** In the final paragraph, the passage is fairly explicit about the role of the reader: to understand the imaginings of the poet. The last sentence of the last paragraph concludes that the "[readers] road leads first into the difficult territory of the poet's imaginings" and only then into the easier and "more familiar world of the poet's words."

   A. While the last paragraph does describe the multiple roles played by the poet, it's not suggested that tension exists in satisfying those roles, or that evidence of multiple roles is apparent in poets' work.

   B. The last sentence of the passage states that understanding the poet's words is easier than placing those words in context of the "poet's imaginings."

   C. While this may or may not be true in real life, the passage doesn't make reference to it. This choice is out of scope.

6. **B is correct.** Answering this question correctly requires an understanding of the critic's role as described in the passage. In keeping with the larger goal being described in this passage—finding those things uniquely common to poets in accomplishing their work—the last paragraph describes how critics can act in this capacity to outline the creative paths followed by poets.

   A. The final paragraph suggests that while critics in the past may have acted, or attempted to act, in this manner, they no longer do.

   C. The author describes the critic and reader as facing similar challenges, but as having different tasks, as the reader must follow ". . . [his] own road."

   D. This may be a tempting response but such a role for a literary critic isn't what's being specifically described in the passage. Instead, the passage conceives of the critic as one who seeks to understand the nature and dimensions of poetry.

7. A is correct. This question asks about the author's intent. Pay close attention to the preceding sentences describing poets' minds moving from specific instances to the general. This is the same as the description of Newton's intellect in the reference sentence. The passage refers to Newton (as an example of another thinker who generalizes from specific examples in the course of a creative process) in order to support the passage's claim that generalization is a quality common to, but not unique to, poets. If Newton, a scientist, generalized from the specific, then, while generalization is held to be an important characteristic of the poet as highlighted by the examples of generalizing poets in the second paragraph, then it can't be unique to the poet. The inclusion of Newton then serves to make the point that generalization is not exclusive to the poetic mind.

    B. No such claim is made. In fact, this sentence draws a parallel between the functioning of the poetic and scientific mind; both the poet and scientist, as represented d by Newton, infer the general from specific instances.

    C. The vivid sense of relation referred to in the opening sentence of the second paragraph is "characteristic" of a poet, but not alone sufficient to define the poetic mind, as others share the characteristic.

    D. In spite of the common use of the word "intellect" in both lines, the reference to Newton's intellect isn't included in order to draw a comparison to the role of the poet as a thinker, but rather to act as a specific example of Newton as a generalizing thinker.

Note-taking Practice Passage II

Bright young scientists must learn through trial-and-error to separate failure to achieve the expected results from failure of the experiment altogether, and when it comes to the latter, technical failures (such as mis-calibrations of instrumentation or other careless oversights) from personal failure. For scientists who are just starting to conduct real research—that is, research in which one does not know what to expect as an outcome, rather than the carefully controlled "experiments" students conduct in the lab solely as a way to learn good lab techniques—a series of setbacks or the failure of a major project can quickly lead to a lack of faith in the experimental process itself. Such failure can create a sense of anxiety over the future of the project, especially in an environment in which the need for funding creates a pressing need to generate positive results quickly. This mental and financial pressure robs the young scientist of the fundamental right of all experimenters: the right to make mistakes. The greatest scientific discoveries have come not after a carefully and elegantly controlled series of pre-planned steps, but rather through the lumpy, uneven process of trial-and-error in which serendipity plays a significant role. But to that scientist who learns the wrong lesson from failure too strongly and too early in their career, the basic enterprise of science ceases to be a learning from failure and instead simply becomes failure.

The scientists' main recourse is to simply recast all lab work as a learning process in which it is the process of experimenting itself that is a success, such that there are no failures. The real sense of oneself as a scientist comes from an ability to understand "failures" as a chance to learn either something about the mechanics of lab work, or something about the system being investigated. The exploration itself becomes the central process of developing the young scientist. If the scientist makes a technical mistake in the operation of a piece of lab equipment, it is an opportunity to develop the toolset that will allow future investigations to proceed more smoothly, whereas if the results are simply wildly different than expected, it gives the scientist an opportunity to investigate something new and interesting about the world. In either case, the central mental faculty being prodded is the scientist's primary tool: curiosity.

An openness and curiosity about the world itself is, of course, the primary motivator for most of those who embark on the scientific journey to begin with. And failure is not always a frustrating setback that many first believe. It was, after all, the failure of Alexander Fleming to properly care for his petri dishes that lead to the discovery of penicillin, or Wilson Greatbach's inadvertent use of a resistor a thousand times too strong that lead to the development of the pacemaker. These sparks of genius and the exhilaration they bring are scattered liberally throughout the entire history of science. Ironically, one of the great curses that can befall a fledgling scientist is to experience not a great stroke of failure at the start of his career, but rather one of these great strokes of luck. If the talented young researcher has such a lucky moment, and comes to believe that such breakthroughs are the normal course of affairs, he may come to think after a subsequent few years of failure that he critically lacks some skill at research and may be driven into a more reliable profession, such as science teaching or science journalism.

Anyone who has devoted their life's work to the laboratory must ultimately have a moment in their career when their curiosity about the research itself, rather than the accolades it may bring, creates a sense of joy. This joy for working in the lab, in which the enterprise ceases to be work and becomes neither a vocation nor an avocation and instead becomes simply a way of life, is the foundational basis for that critical transformation: from a mere technician to a true scientist. Whatever technical mishaps may happen, whatever moments of serendipity may arrive, and whatever the results may show or fail to show, it is the curiosity and joy of discovery that define the scientist.

1. In paragraph three, the author mentions a "failure" of Alexander Fleming and an "inadvertent" action by Wilson Greatbach. In context, these words suggest that at least part of scientific discovery:
   A. requires making technical mistakes.
   B. can only happen to fledgling scientists who have a great stroke of luck.
   C. involves doing things that might typically be considered mistakes.
   D. is motivated by a desire for accolades.

2. The author implies that scientists who persist in their careers as research scientists do so because they:
   A. seek the accolades that come from making a major breakthrough.
   B. are compelled by a sense of curiosity about the world.
   C. would not be happy in a reliable profession such as teaching or journalism.
   D. experience pressure to obtain funding by demonstrating positive results.

3. All of the following are stated in the passage EXCEPT: *maybe*
   A. Making discoveries in the lab creates a sense of curiosity about the world.
   B. Failure to produce positive results quickly can discourage new scientists.
   C. Recasting both technical failures and unexpected results as <u>successes</u> can encourage scientists.
   D. Failure is not always a setback.   (not success)

4. In another work, the author of the passage states that approximately half of promising young Ph.D. candidates who appear as second or third authors on research papers early in their studies eventually either fail to complete their degree or do so without publishing any other original research. This is most likely due to:
   A. new researchers failing to cultivate a sense of curiosity that lets failure be reinterpreted as success.
   B. a stroke of serendipity occurring early in the career of young scientists.
   C. a failure to distinguish between mere technical failures and a failure to achieve the expected results.
   D. a desire to become either a science journalist or a science teacher.

5. One science journalist remarked, "no one likes the blind fumbling about that leads to the lucky discovery; everyone likes having made the lucky discovery". The passage suggests that fledgling scientists who prefer "having made the lucky discovery" might be expected:
   A. to make more lucky discoveries.
   B. to give up research science.
   C. to increase their technical facility in the lab.
   D. to develop a stronger curiosity about the world.

6. The passage most strongly supports which of the following in regards to scientists?
   A. They frequently experience failure through the process of trial-and-error.
   B. Some of the greatest scientists had sloppy lab technique that lead to technical failure.
   C. Whether or not one achieves great success as a scientist depends solely on luck.
   D. Their work transforms who they are by transforming their way of life.

7. Which of the following, if true, would most *weaken* the assertions made by the author?
   A. Scientists should treat the lab as something of a playground in which their imagination can be given free rein.
   B. A scientist prone to technical errors is displaying a personal failure through carelessness and should seek another line of work.
   C. Scientists must cultivate a deep sense of patience since the lucky discovery may come along only after many years.
   D. A scientist is fundamentally an explorer and is at her best when she is off the map: there can be no mistakes because there are no lines to cross.

Note-taking Practice Passage II

Bright young scientists must learn through trial-and-error to separate failure to achieve the expected results from failure of the experiment altogether, and when it comes to the latter, technical failures (such as mis-calibrations of instrumentation or other careless oversights) from personal failure. For scientists who are just starting to conduct real research—that is, research in which one does not know what to expect as an outcome, rather than the carefully controlled "experiments" students conduct in the lab solely as a way to learn good lab techniques—a series of setbacks or the failure of a major project can quickly lead to a lack of faith in the experimental process itself. Such failure can create a sense of anxiety over the future of the project, especially in an environment in which the need for funding creates a pressing need to generate positive results quickly. This mental and financial pressure robs the young scientist of the fundamental right of all experimenters: the right to make mistakes. The greatest scientific discoveries have come not after a carefully and elegantly controlled series of pre-planned steps, but rather through the lumpy, uneven process of trial-and-error in which serendipity plays a significant role. But to that scientist who learns the wrong lesson from failure too strongly and too early in their career, the basic enterprise of science ceases to be a learning from failure and instead simply becomes failure.

Wet-erase Board Notes:

Failing can cause scientists to feel pressured and to give up. Real discovs. from trial-and-error + luck.

The scientists' main recourse is to simply recast all lab work as a learning process in which it is the process of experimenting itself that is a success, such that there are no failures. The real sense of oneself as a scientist comes from an ability to understand "failures" as a chance to learn either something about the mechanics of lab work, or something about the system being investigated. The exploration itself becomes the central process of developing the young scientist. If the scientist makes a technical mistake in the operation of a piece of lab equipment, it is an opportunity to develop the toolset that will allow future investigations to proceed more smoothly, whereas if the results are simply wildly different than expected, it gives the scientist an opportunity to investigate something new and interesting about the world. In either case, the central mental faculty being prodded is the scientist's primary tool: curiosity.

Wet-erase Board Notes:

Auth thinks new sci. need devs. curiosity + see fail as chance to learn.

An openness and curiosity about the world itself is, of course, the primary motivator for most of those who embark on the scientific journey to begin with. And failure is not always a frustrating setback that many first believe. It was, after all, the failure of Alexander Fleming to properly care for his petri dishes that lead to the discovery of penicillin, or Wilson Greatbach's inadvertent use of a resistor a thousand times too strong that lead to the development of the pacemaker. These sparks of genius and the exhilaration they bring are scattered liberally throughout the entire history of science. Ironically, one of the great curses that can befall a fledgling scientist is to experience not a great stroke of failure at the start of his career, but rather one of these great strokes of luck. If the talented young researcher has such a lucky moment, and comes to believe that such breakthroughs are the normal course of affairs, he may come to think after a subsequent few years of failure that he critically lacks some skill at research and may be driven into a more reliable profession, such as science teaching or science journalism.

Wet-erase Board Notes:

Great luck at start of career can be bad. Journalism + teaching more reliable jobs. Curiosity in the first place drives ppl to sci.

Anyone who has devoted their life's work to the laboratory must ultimately have a moment in their career when their curiosity about the research itself, rather than the accolades it may bring, creates a sense of joy. This joy for working in the lab, in which the enterprise ceases to be work and becomes neither a vocation nor an avocation and instead becomes simply a way of life, is the foundational basis for that critical transformation: from a mere technician to a true scientist. Whatever technical mishaps may happen, whatever moments of serendipity may arrive, and whatever the results may show or fail to show, it is the curiosity and joy of discovery that define the scientist.

Wet-erase Board Notes:

Auth.—curiosity and lab research as a way of life def. of true scientist.

Main Idea: The process of becoming a true scientist is one in which native curiosity is channeled into lab work and failures are seen as a chance to learn more.

1. C is correct. The author begins paragraph three by telling us that failure is a part of the scientific process of discovery, and gives us Fleming and Greatbach as examples of that "failure". Choice C matches.
   A. This choice is close but we don't know that Fleming and Greatbach made "technical" mistakes. The more open language of "might" in choice C is better.
   B. "Only" is too strong. We also don't know that Fleming or Greatbach was a fledgling scientist at the time.
   D. We're not told that Fleming or Greatbach sough accolades.

2. B is correct. The overall main theme repeated throughout the passage is one of curiosity driving people into science and then motivating them as scientists. That's choice B.

3. A is the opposite of the author's contention and thus correct. He mentions that being curious is what pushes people into the scientific enterprise in the first place but choice A gets that backwards.
   B. Mentioned in the first paragraph.
   C, D: Mentioned throughout.

4. A is correct. The author's overall theme is that cultivating a curiosity about the world and finding meaning in the lab work itself is what scientists find as the reward, and that this faith in the process itself helps them reinterpret failure as success. If a promising candidate eventually gives up, it most likely indicates choice A: that they haven't been able to develop that ability to recast failure as success.

5. B is correct. The author's main theme throughout is that true scientists come to care more about the process of lab work itself, rather than any accolades that develop. So a young scientist who fails to generate this appreciation for the process itself is unlikely to stick with it.

6. A is correct. The passage tells us right in the first paragraph that science often proceeds through a lumpy uneven process of trial and error. The author mentions this in the context of telling us how often science can generate failure in the lab. This is presented as the normal course of affairs, not something unusual. Thus choice A is true.
   B. We're given examples of some sloppy technique, but those sloppy techniques lead to huge breakthroughs, not to failure.
   C. "Solely" is too extreme here.
   D. This is both too strong and gets the causality backwards. The author tells us that being curious in the first place drives someone to being a scientist, not that being a scientist makes them curious.

7. B is correct. This question asks us to weaken the authors point of view. Choice B is just about the exact opposite of the author's main idea and thus if it were true it would sink the whole passage.
   A, D: These align perfectly with the author's main idea.
   C. The author doesn't directly address patience, but he does emphasize the importance of lucky discoveries. It follows, then, that sticking to it waiting for the lucky discovery is a good trait for scientists.

Approach III: The Skimming Technique

Some students cannot let themselves answer a question without obsessively checking and re-checking the passage. In my decades of MCAT experience, I've learned it's easier to accommodate that particular OCD demon than it is to exorcise it.

Passage: 1-2 minutes

Highlighter: Just key terms—proper nouns, etc.

Wet-erase board: don't use

Question: 8-9 minutes

With the skimming approach, your goal is to zip through the passage, only reading the first couple of lines of each paragraph and the last couple of lines of each paragraph. The idea is to just get a very, very loose general sense of what's going on.

Then get to the questions ASAP. You'll want to read the questions slowly and carefully. Give yourself plenty of time go back and look stuff up. By the time you're done with the question set you'll probably end up reading or re-reading most of the passage.

For the following practice passages, we've slightly greyed-out portions of the passage. We're showing you where you should skim over when you're first reading through the passage. That is, your skim should be focused on the beginnings and ends of paragraphs, and skip over the greyed-out middle of the paragraphs.

This page left intentionally blank.

Skimming Practice Passage I

In his recent book, *The Genius of Dogs: How Dogs are Smarter than You Think*, Brian Hare argues that the communicative abilities of dogs extend well past the blunt signifiers of tail and ear position and bared teeth that humans have long known. If you ask the typical lay person, they would suggest that dog vocalizations consist of little more than barking, growling, and whining. And while Hare's work doesn't expand on this basic repertoire, he convincingly argues that dogs are communicating far more than we were previously aware, through some combination of pitch, loudness and timbre.

Even many dog owners think that a dog's bark contains very little information. That is, the dog isn't "thinking" anything in particular, nor trying to communicate anything in particular. They bark just because "that's what dogs do". Research by Raymond Coppinger seems to support what he calls an "arousal model". That is, dogs simply bark when they're excited about something, and the barking is not a behavior over which the dog is exerting any conscious control and with no attempt at communication by the dog. In support of his hypothesis, Coppinger presents data gathered from several different breeds of working dogs whose job is to protect free-range livestock. In many instances, the dogs barked nearly continuously for six to eight hours, even when no other dogs or humans were within earshot. The bark simply communicates the fact that the barking dog is excited, with no attempt to communicate that message to any particular audience. Hare provides an anecdote which seems to align with the arousal model: he talks about a guard dog he had while working in Africa who would bark at every passerby throughout the night, even when they were people the dog had known and lived with for years.

More recent research, however, suggests that barking and growling may communicate more than had been previously thought. Dogs' vocal cords are highly flexible, permitting dogs to alter their vocalizations to produce a wide variety of different sounds. Scientists recorded the barking and growling done by dogs under a variety of situations. One involved a recording of a "food growl" and a "stranger growl". The first was recorded when researchers attempted to take food away from an aggressive dog, and the second when they simply approached aggressive dogs. They then placed food on the opposite side of the room from another dog and let it approach the food. They played back recordings of both the "stranger" and "food" growls as the dogs approached the food. Only in response to the "food" growl did the dogs hesitate before continuing.

In a similar experiment, researchers recorded the barks of dogs in two different situations. In the first, the dogs were simply left alone. In the second, a stranger would approach the dog, eliciting barking. When those barks were played later for other dogs, these other dogs ignored all of the "alone" barking, but perked up immediately when the "stranger" bark was played. Even more surprising, humans were able to distinguish between the barks, and correctly identify which was which, even if the human test subjects were not themselves dog owners.

Hare also notes that barking behavior itself seems to be an unintended consequence of domestication. While wolves and dogs share many behavioral characteristics (and, in fact, dogs were reclassified in 1993 as a subspecies of wolf), wolves rarely bark. Barking makes up only a small percent—by Hare's estimates as low as 3%—of wolf vocalizations. In addition, the experimental foxes in Russia that have been "force domesticated" over the span of just a handful of generations have shown the same split: the wild-type foxes don't bark, whereas the domesticated ones do. The artificial selection process that selects against aggression and fear in canids seems to have unearthed a propensity for barking.

1. Based on the information in the passage, the presence of barking behavior in the absence of other dogs or humans supports the idea that:
   A. dogs' highly flexible vocal cords permit them to bark for a variety of purposes.
   B. some barking behavior indicates the emotional state of the dog without communicative intent.
   C. the arousal model fails to account for a common observation made by dog owners.
   D. Hare's work is fundamentally flawed.

2. The passage suggests that recordings of dogs barking, to be useful in studying dog communication, must be:
   A. made when attempting to take food away from a dog.
   B. of particularly high quality so as to be recognizable by other dogs.
   C. intelligible to a human audience.
   D. recorded in response to a specific situation being studied.

3. Animal researchers have recorded a set of vocalizations made by hyenas in conjunction with several different hyena behaviors commonly exhibited in the wild. If the researchers wanted to speculate on the function of those vocalizations, Hare would suggest that they:
   A. play those recordings to human listeners and ask the humans to distinguish between the vocalizations.
   B. use a spectrograph to analyze the pitch, loudness, or timbre of the vocalizations.
   C. compare the vocalization behavior of hyenas with their nearest domesticated relative.
   D. play those recordings to other hyenas and observe their reactions.

4. Based on the passage, which of the following pieces of background knowledge would be most helpful in evaluating Hare's contentions?
   A. Knowledge of how vocalization developed as communication tool in people
   B. An understanding of the different sorts of jobs for which dogs have been bred
   C. A familiarity with the normal set of behaviors and vocalizations exhibited by wolves
   D. A familiarity with the skeletal anatomy of a typical dog

5. Which of the following would most strengthen Coppinger's theory about the function of barking?
   A. There are perceptible differences in the barks of dogs who are being threatened by larger animals and those being threatened by smaller animals.
   B. When fed a slight sedative, the barking activity of dogs tended to increase in response to strangers.
   C. Wolves show an increased amount of barking when kept in captivity.
   D. When given food that contained small doses of stimulant drugs but provided with no environmental cues, dogs increased the duration and frequency of their barking.

Skimming Practice Passage I

In his recent book, *The Genius of Dogs: How Dogs are Smarter than You Think*, Brian Hare argues that the communicative abilities of dogs extend well past the blunt signifiers of tail and ear position and bared teeth that humans have long known. If you ask the typical lay person, they would suggest that dog vocalizations consist of little more than barking, growling, and whining. And while Hare's work doesn't expand on this basic repertoire, he convincingly argues that dogs are communicating far more than we were previously aware, through some combination of pitch, loudness and timbre.

Even many dog owners think that a dog's bark contains very little information. That is, the dog isn't "thinking" anything in particular, nor trying to communicate anything in particular. They bark just because "that's what dogs do". Research by Raymond Coppinger seems to support what he calls an "arousal model". That is, dogs simply bark when they're excited about something, and the barking is not a behavior over which the dog is exerting any conscious control and with no attempt at communication by the dog. In support of his hypothesis, Coppinger presents data gathered from several different breeds of working dogs whose job is to protect free-range livestock. In many instances, the dogs barked nearly continuously for six to eight hours, even when no other dogs or humans were within earshot. The bark simply communicates the fact that the barking dog is excited, with no attempt to communicate that message to any particular audience. Hare provides an anecdote which seems to align with the arousal model: he talks about a guard dog he had while working in Africa who would bark at every passerby throughout the night, even when they were people the dog had known and lived with for years.

More recent research, however, suggests that barking and growling may communicate more than had been previously thought. Dogs' vocal cords are highly flexible, permitting dogs to alter their vocalizations to produce a wide variety of different sounds. Scientists recorded the barking and growling done by dogs under a variety of situations. One involved a recording of a "food growl" and a "stranger growl". The first was recorded when researchers attempted to take food away from an aggressive dog, and the second when they simply approached aggressive dogs. They then placed food on the opposite side of the room from another dog and let it approach the food. They played back recordings of both the "stranger" and "food" growls as the dogs approached the food. Only in response to the "food" growl did the dogs hesitate before continuing.

In a similar experiment, researchers recorded the barks of dogs in two different situations. In the first, the dogs were simply left alone. In the second, a stranger would approach the dog, eliciting barking. When those barks were played later for other dogs, these other dogs ignored all of the "alone" barking, but perked up immediately when the "stranger" bark was played. Even more surprising, humans were able to distinguish between the barks, and correctly identify which was which, even if the human test subjects were not themselves dog owners.

Hare also notes that barking behavior itself seems to be an unintended consequence of domestication. While wolves and dogs share many behavioral characteristics (and, in fact, dogs were reclassified in 1993 as a subspecies of wolf), wolves rarely bark. Barking makes up only a small percent—by Hare's estimates as low as 3%—of wolf vocalizations. In addition, the experimental foxes in Russia that have been "force domesticated" over the span of just a handful of generations have shown the same split: the wild-type foxes don't bark, whereas the domesticated ones do. The artificial selection process that selects against aggression and fear in canids seems to have unearthed a propensity for barking.

Main Idea: Dog vocalizations communicate more than we previously thought, and although dogs sometimes bark in response to general excitement, they are capable of barking to communicate a variety of different situations.

1. B is correct. The question makes specific reference to an example of dog barking from Coppinger's studies. As Coppinger stated, dogs bark in response to general arousal (emotional state) without communicating anything in particular, as choice B says.

2. D is correct. In analyzing the various types of barking, the researches played the recordings of the barking back for other dogs to hear and for other humans. So both choice B and C seem tempting, but we can eliminate them both. After all, if C were correct, then B would also have to be correct. You can't have two right answers! Instead, we have to think not about who the recordings were played for, but when and why they were recorded—in response to different situations. Choice D nails it.

3. D is correct. We must apply the technique used in the passage to a new situation. In the passage, the study was done by recording a dog's barks and then playing those barks back to listeners—first other dogs, then people who interact with dogs. A similar protocol would be choice D, to play hyena vocalizations back for other hyenas.

4. C is correct. The passage tells us that dogs are a subset of wolves, and Hare contends that barking serves as a communication tool, with different types of barks associated with different types of behaviors or situations. A relevant set of background data would be how wolves vocalize in response to different situations.

5. A, B, D: These are all only very tangentially related to dog vocalization.

6. D is correct. Coppinger's theory was that barking simply indicates arousal. Thus he would suggest that feeding dogs a stimulant would lead to more barking behavior, even in the absence of any particular signals from people or other dogs. Choice D nails it.
   A. This suggests communication by the dog, which is the opposite of Coppinger's theory.
   B. This is the opposite of what Coppinger would suggest. A sedative would reduce arousal.

Skimming Practice Passage II

As one looks forward to the <u>America</u> of fifty years hence, the main source of anxiety appears to be in a probable <u>excess of prosperity</u>, and in the want of a good grievance. We seem nearly at the end of those great public wrongs which require a special moral earthquake to end them. There seems nothing left which need be absolutely fought for; no great influence to keep us from a commonplace and perhaps debasing success. There will, no doubt, be still need of the statesman to adjust the details of government, and of the clergyman to keep an eye on private morals, including his own. There will also be social and religious changes, perhaps great ones; but there are no omens of any very fierce upheaval. And seeing the educational value to this generation of the reforms for which it has contended, one must feel an impulse of pity for our successors, who seem likely to have no convictions that they can honestly be mobbed for.

Can we spare these great tonics? It is the experience of history that all religious bodies are purified by persecution, and materialized by peace. No amount of accumulated virtue has thus far saved the merely devout communities from deteriorating, when let alone, into comfort and good dinners. This is most noticeable in detached organizations,—Moravians, Shakers, Quakers, Roman Catholics,—they all go the same way at last; when persecution and missionary toil are over, they enter on a tiresome millennium of meat and pudding. To guard against this spiritual obesity, this carnal Eden, what has the next age in reserve for us? Suppose however many million perfectly healthy and virtuous Americans, what is to keep them from being as uninteresting as so many Chinese?

I know of nothing but that aim which is the climax and flower of all civilization, without which purity itself grows dull and devotion tedious,—the pursuit of Science and Art. Give to all this nation peace, freedom, prosperity, and even virtue, still there must be some absorbing interest, some career. That career can be sought only in two directions—more and yet more material prosperity on the one side. Science and Art on the other. Every man's aim must either be riches, or something better than riches. To advocate the alternative career, the striving of the whole nature after something utterly apart from this world's wealth,—it is for this end that a stray voice is needed. It will not take long; the clamor of the market will re-absorb us to-morrow.

[Adapted from "Literature as an Art", *The Atlantic Monthly*, December, 1867.]

1. The author's primary purpose in this passage is:
   A. to provide a call to arms for individuals to follow passionate, challenging lives.
   B. to draw attention to the dramatic irony of a society starved for evil.
   C. to acknowledge the death of art as the bittersweet but necessary price of peace and justice.
   D. to argue for Science and Art as the inevitable flower and final purpose of a mature civilization.

2. Which of the following, if true, would most *weaken* the passage author's main argument?
   A. Moravians, Quakers, and Roman Catholics are found to have most increased their prosperity in peacetime.
   B. During the last US-involved war, sculpture increased while live theater decreased.
   C. Hemingway's greatest novel, *A Farewell to Arms*, was based on his experiences in the Great War.
   D. A national survey shows that individuals insulated from social upheaval are rated as the most passionate.

3. Which of the following assumptions does the author make in the first paragraph?
   A. Challenging but laudable tasks benefit those who undertake them.
   B. Later generations are as likely to have strong moral convictions as the current one.
   C. A strong moral imperative can be gained from experience.
   D. Moral conviction is less desirable than an easy life.

4. According to the passage, which of the following exemplifies the decline of a people or organization after its battles are won and trials endured?
   A. The safe, boring lives of millions of Chinese.
   B. The debasing success of America's latest moral earthquake.
   C. The Shaker's post-missionary-phase millennium of prosperity.
   D. The increase of peacetime science.

5. Which of the following does the passage author assume to be true, based on the second paragraph?
   A. China has never experienced war or serious social upheaval.
   B. Hard-earned virtue is preferable to meaningless ease.
   C. The Quakers have become materialistic and complacent.
   D. Pudding is contradictory to revolution.

6. In context, when the passage describes a "spiritual obesity, a carnal Eden", the author means
   A. that without some bitterness in life, the sweet can never be as sweet.
   B. that an excess of prosperity can lead to spiritual ill-health.
   C. that paradise on Earth is a part of humanity's future, rather than its past.
   D. that austerity, not prosperity, is necessary for moral uprightness.

7. Suppose a survey of Spanish poetry from the 13th to 21st century revealed the frequency of highly-acclaimed and widely reprinted work (relative to the amount published during the period) spiked during revolutionary periods. The passage author would likely explain this as
   A. the result of unjust circumstances fostering a passion for truth and moral right.
   B. a result of the lack of lucrative employment making the arts more desirable.
   C. an anomaly, explainable by the heterogeneity of a nation in crisis.
   D. a result of a greater demand for beautiful things in difficult times.

Skimming Practice Passage II

As one looks forward to the America of fifty years hence, the main source of anxiety appears to be in a probable excess of prosperity, and in the want of a good grievance. We seem nearly at the end of those great public wrongs which require a special moral earthquake to end them. There seems nothing left which need be absolutely fought for; no great influence to keep us from a commonplace and perhaps debasing success. There will, no doubt, be still need of the statesman to adjust the details of government, and of the clergyman to keep an eye on private morals, including his own. There will also be social and religious changes, perhaps great ones; but there are no omens of any very fierce upheaval. And seeing the educational value to this generation of the reforms for which it has contended, one must feel an impulse of pity for our successors, who seem likely to have no convictions that they can honestly be mobbed for.

Can we spare these great tonics? It is the experience of history that all religious bodies are purified by persecution, and materialized by peace. No amount of accumulated virtue has thus far saved the merely devout communities from deteriorating, when let alone, into comfort and good dinners. This is most noticeable in detached organizations,—Moravians, Shakers, Quakers, Roman Catholics,—they all go the same way at last; when persecution and missionary toil are over, they enter on a tiresome millennium of meat and pudding. To guard against this spiritual obesity, this carnal Eden, what has the next age in reserve for us? Suppose however many million perfectly healthy and virtuous Americans, what is to keep them from being as uninteresting as so many Chinese?

I know of nothing but that aim which is the climax and flower of all civilization, without which purity itself grows dull and devotion tedious,—the pursuit of Science and Art. Give to all this nation peace, freedom, prosperity, and even virtue, still there must be some absorbing interest, some career. That career can be sought only in two directions—more and yet more material prosperity on the one side. Science and Art on the other. Every man's aim must either be riches, or something better than riches. To advocate the alternative career, the striving of the whole nature after something utterly apart from this world's wealth,—it is for this end that a stray voice is needed. It will not take long; the clamor of the market will re-absorb us to-morrow.

[Adapted from "Literature as an Art", *The Atlantic Monthly*, December, 1867.]

Main Idea: a society with no injustice, no pain, no evil, is at risk of losing its greatness, so one must advocate the pursuit of greatness through art and science

1. A is correct. At first glance, A , B, and C all seem relatively close matches for the main idea of the passage. D is almost exactly lifted from the passage, and is found in the concluding paragraph, however it doesn't fully encapsulate the main idea. However, it does show why A is the best match. The passage author not only elucidates the problem of a society with no more physical or moral battles to fight, he advocates a solution, which A is a reasonably good match for. He does not discuss the problem merely to make a point of its irony (B), nor to reluctantly accept it as an inevitability (C).

2. D is correct. The main argument is that great societal challenges such as war or social injustices that need changing provide a sort of moral education for the citizens who experience and face these great tasks, and, as a corollary, that the lack of such crises denies individuals the opportunity to learn virtue and conviction. Either evidence of a society with great challenges but little moral conviction, or a society without such challenges whose citizens nevertheless have great moral conviction, would weaken the argument. D is a pretty good match for the latter and, if true, would weaken the main argument. Both A and B are neutral, neither strengthening nor weakening the main argument, while C actually strengthens it.

3. C is correct. A is not an assumption but an explicit statement. B is contrary to what the passage suggests in the first paragraph. But the first paragraph notes the educational value of the fight for reforms, stating that those who come later, in the peaceful era, will lack conviction. The implication is that the lack of such experiences will be responsible for the lack of conviction, which assumes that moral conviction can be learned, matching the statement in C. D is the exact opposite of another assumption the author makes, given the comment about pitying those who come later.

4. C is correct. Since the question stem specifically asks about the decline of a people, the answer choice must reflect the time of stability after all the battles are won. There was no mention in the passage itself of what previous trials and tribulations the Chinese have or have not faced, so A can be eliminated. America's recent social upheaveal is mentioned, but the expected decline is hypothetical and lies still in the future, so B is not a good match either. C is a perfect match, and is found in the passage. D is offered in the passage as a cure for such a decline, not a sign of it.

5. B is correct. Since the answer choices come from different parts of the paragraph, it's necessary to examine them one at a time. A is very tempting, as the author compares citizens of a turbulent America to those of China, suggesting that the latter country has been stable and free of war (and its citizens consequently boring). However, this does not necessarily mean that the country has never faced war or upheaval, only that it has not in the most recent generation at the time the passage was written. B, however, is assumed, given the tone of the passage. In this paragraph, the passage author describes a life of peace and material ease as tiresome, deteriorated, and boring. The author is operating under the assumption that such a life is undesirable. C is a consequence of that same assumption, and is outright stated, not assumed. D might be tempting, but on closer examination it is not integral to the argument. Although pudding is used as an example or indicator of sloth and complacency, it's not the main point. The author is not arguing against eating pudding, but against a life where everything is easy and passion has no place. It's not necessary to assume that a revolutionary cannot have the occasional pudding.

6. B is correct. The author's colorful phrasing, a "spiritual obesity", uses the metaphor of overindulgence causing ill health to describe the surprising results of achieving prosperity and peace. The purpose of the passage is to warn against this danger, and the purpose of the quoted phrase is to sum up the problem, which is well-stated in B. Answer choice A sounds reasonable based on the phrasing itself, but does not match any of the arguments in the passage. C, too, is nowhere in the passage. D is tempting, as it nearly hits the passage author's main idea, but the problem is not the lack of "lack", but the lack of an actual injustice or challenge. The focus on prosperity versus austerity misses the mark somewhat.

7. A is correct. The passage author's main argument describes social turbulence and injustice as moral teachers, and the lack of them as leading to a bland, convictionless populace. It follows that individuals of passion and moral strength are disproportionately created—taught—during turbulent times. It's assumed that this creates better and more meaningful art. A is a good match for this. B is nowhere in the passage. C contradicts the main idea, which predicts this outcome rather than calling it an anomaly. D too is not in the passage.

3. Must-Knows

> There's no such thing as a "right way" to tackle the CARS passages—only *your* right way.
> - To figure out your right way, start practicing passages right away. Use resources such as Next Step's Review books, online Full Lengths, or AAMC resources to get the practice you need.
> There are three main approaches to CARS passages:
> - Note-taking involves a slower, more careful analysis of the passage and jotting down key ideas as you read. If you take this approach, you will have to move more quickly through the questions.
> - Highlighting is a balanced approach where you spend a little less than half your time on the passage and a little more than half your time on the questions. This tends to be the most popular approach.
> - Skimming means quickly looking over the first and last sentence of each paragraph and getting to the questions in under a minute. While this approach can save a bunch of time, it relies heavily on an exceptionally good ability to skim the passage looking for information relevant to the question.

Analyzing CARS Questions

0. Introduction

Once you've gotten a handle on how to tackle the passages, you should start to hone your approach to the questions. The AAMC divides CARS questions into three categories: foundations of comprehension, reasoning within the text, and reasoning beyond the text. These three types each represent about 1/3 of the questions you'll see on Test Day.

Although questions can vary tremendously in length, subtlety, and difficulty, they should all be approached with the same basic rhythm. While it's certainly possible to develop a complex hierarchy of seventeen different question types and craft an arcane multi-step method that will supposedly provide the "trick" needed to get every question right, the simple truth is that answering questions correctly depends much more on an excellent understanding of the passage followed by an approach that keeps you focused on the only issues that matter—*exactly* what did they ask you and *exactly* what did the passage have to say on the issue?

When actually facing the CARS section on Test Day, we want to make sure our minds are clear to focus on the passage and the exact wording of the question, not some complex method. Thus, the Next Step approach to the questions is less a "method" and more a simple rhythm.

1. Read/Rephrase/Research/Respond

The rhythm to follow involves first reading the question (of course!) and then stopping for a beat. Take a breath, and think over what the question just asked you. Mentally rephrase it. "What is the question really asking me?"

After you've understood the question, then do the research—somewhere in the passage, in your highlighting, or in your notes is the information you need. How exactly you carry out this research will depend on your approach to the passage itself.

Finally, respond to the question. You may have a very good idea of exactly what you need, so you'll have a mental prediction and you can whiz through the choices

> **MCAT STRATEGY > > >**
>
> Know and practice the basic rhythm for tackling a question: Read, Rephrase, Research, and Respond. You want this to be so ingrained that by Test Day you do it without having to stop to think about it.

looking to match your prediction. Alternatively, you may not know exactly what they want, so you do a process of elimination.

2. CARS Practice

On the following pages are five practice passages. Use these passages as a chance to both work on your passage reading technique (whether that's highlighting, note-taking, or skimming) and your rhythm for answering the questions.

Whenever you get a question wrong, go back and analyze where things went wrong. Did you fail to read the *exact* wording of the question? Rephrase it to understand it? Did your research find the relevant information? When responding to the question, did the choice you selected actually match what your research showed? Careful analysis is the key to improving your performance.

This page left intentionally blank.

CARS Practice Passage 1

There are two fundamental types of control. The first of these is external, in which a person attempts to exert agency upon the world by controlling other people and, by extension, events outside the self. Such personality types are quite common, and can readily be seen in everything from the schoolyard bully to the sociopathic corporate CEO to the screaming drill sergeant.

The second type of control, however, is the one that ultimately brings greater self-empowerment and often, ironically, greater influence over external events. In this second type—internal control—a person does not seek to directly change the behavior of other people. Instead, the individual seeks total mastery over personal reactions, both cognitive and emotional, to the environment. Such an individual can then, through force of positive example, end up controlling other people. *[handwritten: 2 types of control external + internal / Bully, control others / more control]*

In the majority culture of the United States, the first type of control is presented as the dominant narrative. Many of America's greatest cultural successes have come in the form of a person or a group of people actively working to change the world around them. America's dominant cultural paradigm is that of the scientist and the technological innovator working together to first discover, and then to exploit the laws of the natural world in a way that creates greater and greater control by humanity over nature. Historians draw a straight line from the investigations of Benjamin Franklin to the great 19th century inventors of Fulton, Whitney, and Morse to the technical mastery of Edison and the industrial genius of Ford. Perhaps the culmination of this worldview was the 1960's space race in which the American mindset of domination over nature put a man on the moon—still one of the most startling technological achievements in human history.

Those who wish to argue for the value of internal control face an uphill battle. When it is suggested that dominating the external world is ultimately a self-defeating process, most who listen will scoff. After all, can we not see the great riches of the businessman who dominates his competition? Are not the problems created by technological domination solved through technological means? The fundamental problems of external control seem mere by-products when they are not missed entirely.

The profound problem created by external control is that, by its very nature, it must create more losers than winners. If a business enterprise consists of a dozen competing sales representatives and only one of them can win the bonus for highest number of sales, then the "game" is rigged to create eleven losers. So it is too with technological domination over nature. If humanity's successful external control of nature makes us the winner, then every other species on Earth must be the loser (or in the case of domesticated species, relegated to a bland, bleached-out second place existence). The structure of external control social systems would seem to suggest to most participants that it is not in their best interests. For any one person, the odds of being a loser in an external control system is higher than being the lone winner. And yet rarely are people willing to shift their worldview when faced with this stark fact. Even after failing to successfully exert external control over and over, they simply blame their failure on bad luck or some other extenuating circumstance. *[handwritten: external control = bad → people still use it/like it]*

Ultimately, it is through examination of the greatest successes of external control that we may see the seeds for a successful argument for turning our vision inward. Time after time, when those who have gained great success through controlling others are interviewed near the end of their lives, they admit to the hollowness of their success. With little searching, we can uncover any number of autobiographies in which great and "powerful" people express regret over their lifestyle and come to realize in the end that their basic attitude toward the world, although generating short-term success, failed to create the true happiness and success that can only be attained by those whose control is turned inward.

1. The assertion that historians draw a straight line from Ben Franklin to the Space Race is:
   A. true, on the basis of intervening successive technological achievements by other American inventors.
   B. supported by examples in the passage.
   C. possible but not supported by direct examples in the passage.
   D. false based on the author's conclusion that internal control is ultimately more successful.

2. The author's conclusion about external control and American society would be most *weakened* if which of the following were found to be true?
   A. A majority of working Americans describe their working lives as "collaborative" and their relations with their neighbors as "cooperative".
   B. In behavioral studies of group dynamics, most Americans will adopt a "dominating" stance and will continue to believe that that is the best strategy even after failing to achieve objectives.
   C. American sports that focus on competition with a sole winner, such as golf or tennis, are vastly more popular than cooperative sports such as hiking or mountain climbing.
   D. Only 5% of American adults categorize themselves as "technically adept" and answer "yes" when asked, "Do you eagerly look forward to new inventions and technology?"

3. The author implies that if the writer of a self-help book advocates internal control as the best way to approach life, many American readers would:
   A. go to great lengths to shift how they attempt to exercise control in their lives.
   B. read the book carefully and then offer a dispassionate, carefully reasoned argument to prove the writer wrong.
   C. refuse to shift their worldview and simply conclude that the writer was wrong.
   D. be curious enough to explore the idea further.

4. One can infer that if a new corporation structured its employees along external-control lines in which a small number of "winning" employees were disproportionately rewarded, the company's workforce would:
   A. believe that such a structure is in their best interests.
   B. believe that such a structure is not in their best interests.
   C. feel so discontent that many would quit or retire early.
   D. take such a structure for granted.

5. The author believes that technology is relevant to the distinction between internal and external control as expressed in American culture because:
   I. technology permits improved human welfare and happiness.
   II. it facilitates a winner versus loser dichotomy that reflects the two types of control.
   III. opposing technologic domination garners a dismissive reaction.
   A. II only
   B. III only
   C. I and II only
   D. II and III only

6. A study demonstrating that most parents in the U.S. attempt to shape their children's behavior by telling the children what to do would:
   A. support the author's point that Americans tend to favor external control.
   B. support the author's main idea only if most parents also attempt to shape their children's behavior by setting a good example for them.
   C. directly contradict one of the author's supporting points, but not the main point.
   D. weaken the assertion that people failing at external control blame bad luck rather than the external control mindset.

CARS Practice Passage 1

There are two fundamental types of control. The first of these is external, in which a person attempts to exert agency upon the world by controlling other people and, by extension, events outside the self. Such personality types are quite common, and can readily be seen in everything from the schoolyard bully to the sociopathic corporate CEO to the screaming drill sergeant.

Key terms: control, external

Opinion: External control tries to directly control events outside the self and is quite common

The second type of control, however, is the one that ultimately brings greater self-empowerment and often, ironically, greater influence over external events. In this second type—internal control—a person does not seek to directly change the behavior of other people. Instead, the individual seeks total mastery over personal reactions, both cognitive and emotional, to the environment. Such an individual can then, through force of positive example, end up controlling other people.

Contrast: external control vs. internal control

Opinion: Author thinks internal control leads to great self-empowerment, greater influence

Cause and effect: Internal control lets you set a good example which ultimately leads to greater influence.

In the majority culture of the United States, the first type of control is presented as the dominant narrative. Many of America's greatest cultural successes have come in the form of a person or a group of people actively working to change the world around them. America's dominant cultural paradigm is that of the scientist and the technological innovator working together to first discover, and then to exploit the laws of the natural world in a way that creates greater and greater control by humanity over nature. Historians may draw a straight line from the investigations of Benjamin Franklin to the great 19th century inventors of Fulton, Whitney, and Morse to the technical mastery of Edison and the industrial genius of Ford. Perhaps the culmination of this worldview was the 1960's space race in which the American mindset of domination over nature put a man on the moon—still one of the most startling technological achievements in human history.

Key terms: United states, Franklin, Fulton, Whitney, Morse, Edison, Ford, space race

Opinion: Author sees US as favoring an external control model, primarily through its favoring science and technological advancement.

Those who wish to argue for the value of internal control face an uphill battle. When it is suggested that dominating the external world is ultimately a self-defeating process, most who listen will scoff. After all, can we not see the great riches of the businessman who dominates his competition? Are not the problems created by technological domination solved through technological means? The fundamental problems of external control seem mere by-products when they are not missed entirely.

Opinion: Author thinks most will just scoff or ignore calls for internal control, since people either miss the problems of external control entirely, or think that the problems it creates are solved by more of the same.

The profound problem created by external control is that, by its very nature, it must create more losers than winners. If a business enterprise consists of a dozen competing sales representatives and only one of them can win the bonus for highest number of sales, then the "game" is rigged to create eleven losers. So it is too with technological domination over nature. If humanity's successful external control of nature makes us the winner, then every other species on Earth must be the loser (or in the case of domesticated species, relegated to a bland, bleached-out second place existence). The structure of external control social systems would seem to suggest to most participants that it is not in their best interests. For any one person, the odds of being a loser in an external control system is higher than being the lone winner. And yet rarely are people willing to shift their worldview when faced with this stark fact. Even after failing to successfully exert external control over and over, they simply blame their failure on bad luck or some other extenuating circumstance.

Cause and effect: External control systems are rigged to create more losers than winners

Opinion: Author thinks that people can't change their views, and even after losing repeatedly will just blame bad luck rather than change their outlook.

Ultimately, it is through examination of the greatest successes of external control that we may see the seeds for a successful argument for turning our vision inward. Time after time, when those who have gained great success through controlling others are interviewed near the end of their lives, they admit to the hollowness of their success. With little searching, we can uncover any number of autobiographies in which great and "powerful" people express regret over their lifestyle and come to realize in the end that their basic attitude toward the world, although generating short-term success, failed to create the true happiness and success that can only be attained by those whose control is turned inward.

Opinion: Author thinks that by looking at the deathbed regrets of those few "winners" who were created by external control systems we see the basic problem—that it leads to hollowness and dissatisfaction.

Main Idea: Despite the overwhelming preference of Americans for an external-control view of the world, it is ultimately internal control that creates more happiness, more success, and ironically more control over the external world.

1. B is correct. The author cites several examples of inventors and technological innovators when moving from Franklin to the space race—Fulton, Morse, etc.

2. A is correct. To weaken the author's view we need to see that Americans aren't interested in a world view in which they dominate the external environment and control it.
    B. This would support the author's view that Americans take an external control, dominating stance to dealing with the world.
    C. The popularity of sports that involve a sole winner and many losers (as opposed to noncompetitive sports like hiking) would support the author's view.
    D. Technology was merely an analogy for the types of control, and the lack of tech savvy among lay people doesn't directly address the question.

3. C is correct. The author tells us that Americans would scoff at such a book, or miss the problems of external control entirely. They just don't want to change their world view.

4. D is correct. We're told that Americans just assume that an external control system that creates few winners and many loser is simply accepted by most, and that even when they end up as the loser they can't see the problem—they just blame bad luck. Thus they would take such a system for granted.

5. D is correct. The author discusses technology as an example of the American cultural preference for external control. We're told that Americans will dismiss the idea that there's anything wrong with external control (the problems created by technological domination are solved by more technology). II and III both fit the author's main idea and reflect his arguments about external control.

6. A is correct. Directly giving a child an order telling them what to do would be the perfect archetype of external control.

CARS Practice Passage 2

There are many who acknowledge that the political structures of the day have an influence of the development of literature but vehemently oppose the notion that a subtle biological evolution of the brain has anything to do with the matter. Yet consider the difference between the forms of literature created by pre-literate societies in ancient times and those made during and after the Industrial revolution: each exhibits a stark contrast with the other, and the production, consumption, and goals of such literature have a subtle interplay not just with the political ecology in which they were created, but on the kind of brain intended to receive the literary message.

brains have maybe evolved → literature reflects this

Pre-literate societies had to transmit their literature orally, whereas industrialized societies did so in writing. The primary mental tool by which oral literature is both transmitted and consumed is memory, which requires development of the hippocampus and amygdala. Reading literature, however, triggers a series of mechanical controls for the eyes, and in the brain's visual processing centers in the occipital lobe, bypassing much of the memory activation centers.

preliterate → memory
writing → mechanical

It may seem absurd that the biological evolution of the brain influences the sorts of literature produced, and yet when neuroimaging studies are done on the brains of present-day peoples whose cultures most nearly approximate ancient ways of living, they reveal strong differences in both structural and functional development from contemporary brains.

study

Surviving for millennia as hunter-gatherers required the development a brain with an astounding spatial memory. Early humans roved over vast territories in their search for food, and they had to be able to store this data and recall it effortlessly in order to survive. This lifestyle both selected for and subsequently promoted the neural architecture for memory. It is unsurprising, then, that the literature developed under such circumstances would depend heavily on memory. This memory-based literature persisted long after agriculture and civilization became the predominant mode of living; the ancient Greeks were well known to equate memory with intelligence itself. By contrast, once man developed systems for externalizing memory (first the written word, then later recorded sound and images), the primary mental virtue became speed of processing that information. Thus the literature that developed from medieval times onward tended towards exceptionally lengthy tomes that the reader would move through relatively quickly.

preliterate → memory = intelligence   architecture memory for survival
later ability to recall = new evolution

These differences are not merely technological or cultural. The neuroimaging studies done on "ancient peoples" were extended to comparing the brains of infants less than a week old. Those children born in industrial and post-industrial societies already showed stronger initial development of visual processing and prefrontal cortical regions whereas infants in pre-agricultural tribal societies (most notably the Etoro people of Papua New Guinea and the Pano tribe in the Amazon rainforest) had more well developed hippocampal and amygdalar architectures.

differences aren't based on surroundings

It is speculated that these difference also relate to the functions that literature develops in each situation: in pre-literate societies, the oral transmission of a culture's stories also functions to develop a mindfulness about the environment in which the listeners find themselves. These stories seek to inculcate traditional values. Modern literature, on the other hand, tends to serve mostly as a distraction from the environment. The entertainment value of the work crowds out other possible meanings.

preliterate = engages enviro
post = distract from enviro

The central fact that both forms of literature have in common, however, is the assumption that the creator of the literature—either the author of the novel in one case, or the reciter of the story in the other—shares the same basic framework of neural architecture as the listener.

1. In the fifth paragraph, the "differences" the author mentions refer to:
   A. the differences in the speed with which literature is consumed in different societies.
   B. the fact that literature serves very different social functions in pre-literate and industrialized societies.
   C. the differences in neuroanatomy that are correlated with different forms of literature.
   D. minor differences in neural architecture between the creator and consumer of literature.

2. The author suggests that the consumption of literature in contemporary society:
   A. increases development in most areas of the brain.
   B. decreases environmental awareness while not conveying deeper meanings.
   C. is motivated by a desire to develop visual processing ability.
   D. encourages a slower, more careful evaluation of the meanings of printed words.

3. The author asserts that children born in modern societies have more advanced prefrontal cortical regions (which are associated with careful, reasoned judgments that take time to make) but also consume literature in a way that rewards speed of information processing. Are these two assertions reconcilable?
   A. Yes; the author makes no assertions that would prevent a particular type of literature from contributing to the development of areas of the brain with disparate functions.
   B. Yes; faster information processing requires more careful judgment about what parts of that information are important.
   C. No; the close relationship between increased processing speed and written forms of literature is incompatible with slowed brain activity.
   D. No; careful, reasoned judgments are the antithesis of the kind of brain activity described by the author.

4. When the author asserts in paragraph four that a certain lifestyle selected for the neural architecture of memory, the author means that:
   A. a lifestyle that required an exceptionally strong memory promoted the survival of the offspring of parents with well-developed hippocampal and amygdalar architectures.
   B. those individuals with well-developed memories selected a lifestyle that rewarded them for having a strong memory.
   C. ancient Greek civilizations rewarded those with strong memories.
   D. hunter-gatherers developed their memory throughout their lives.

5. Which of the following, if true, would most clearly *disprove* the author's thesis?
   A. Comprehension and appreciation of literature is enhanced when the creator and consumer of the literature have similar physiological and sociological backgrounds.
   B. The type of literature we consume can influence how our brains develop.
   C. When children from pre-literate societies are brought to schools and taught to read, they are able to develop a proficiency at reading that is roughly similar to children from literate societies.
   D. Widespread genetic testing of human remains demonstrates that no evolution has taken place in *homo sapiens* over the past 50,000 years.

CARS Practice Passage 2

There are many who acknowledge that the political structures of the day have an influence of the development of literature but vehemently oppose the notion that a subtle biological evolution of the brain has anything to do with the matter. Yet consider the difference between the forms of literature created by pre-literate societies in ancient times and those made during and after the Industrial revolution: each exhibits a stark contrast with the other, and the production, consumption, and goals of such literature have a subtle interplay not just with the political ecology in which they were created, but on the kind of brain intended to receive the literary message.

Key terms: political structures, industrial revolution

Opinion: Many wouldn't think evolution of brain affects literature

Contrast: pre-literate and industrial societies have differing literature

Pre-literate societies had to transmit their literature orally, whereas industrialized societies did so in writing. The primary mental tool by which oral literature is both transmitted and consumed is memory, which requires development of the hippocampus and amygdala. Reading literature, however, triggers a series of mechanical controls for the eyes, and in the brain's visual processing centers in the occipital lobe, bypassing much of the memory activation centers.

Key terms: amygdala, hippocampus, occipital lob

Contrast: oral literature depends on memory, written literature is more visual

It may seem absurd that the biological evolution of the brain influences the sorts of literature produced, and yet when neuroimaging studies are done on the brains of present-day peoples whose cultures most nearly approximate ancient ways of living, they reveal strong differences in both structural and functional development from contemporary brains.

Key terms: neuroimaging studies

Contrast: the brains of pre-literate and industrial people are different

Surviving for millennia as hunter-gatherers required the development a brain with an astounding spatial memory. Early humans roved over vast territories in their search for food, and they had to be able to store this data and recall it effortlessly in order to survive. This lifestyle both selected for and subsequently promoted the neural architecture for memory. It is unsurprising, then, that the literature developed under such circumstances would depend heavily on memory. This memory-based literature persisted long after agriculture and civilization became the predominant mode of living; the ancient Greeks were well known to equate memory with intelligence itself. By contrast, once man developed systems for externalizing memory (first the written word, then later recorded sound and images), the primary mental virtue became speed of processing that information. Thus the literature that developed from medieval times onward tended towards exceptionally lengthy tomes that the reader would move through relatively quickly.

Key terms: hunter-gatherers, spatial memory, ancient Greeks

Contrast: hunter-gatherers depends on excellent memory for survival but literate societies values quick processing over memory

These differences are not merely technological or cultural. The neuroimaging studies done on "ancient peoples" were extended to comparing the brains of infants less than a week old. Those children born in industrial and post-industrial societies already showed stronger initial development of visual processing and prefrontal cortical regions whereas infants in pre-agricultural tribal societies (most notably the Etoro people of Papua New Guinea and the Pano tribe in the Amazon rainforest) had more well developed hippocampal and amygdalar architectures.

Key terms: Etoro, Pano, hippocampal, amygdalar

Contrast: Even in infants a week old, there are already differences in the brains of "ancient peoples" and modern ones.

It is speculated that these difference also relate to the functions that literature develops in each situation: in pre-literate societies, the oral transmission of a culture's stories also functions to develop a mindfulness about the environment in which the listeners find themselves. These stories seek to inculcate traditional values. Modern literature, on the other hand, tends to serve mostly as a distraction from the environment. The entertainment value of the work crowds out other possible meanings.

Key terms: function, mindfulness, distraction

Contrast: Literature in oral cultures encourages mindfulness but in modern culture is for entertainment and distraction.

The central fact that both forms of literature have in common, however, is the assumption that the creator of the literature—either the author of the novel in one case, or the reciter of the story in the other—shares the same basic framework of neural architecture as the listener.

Opinion: The author thinks the basic assumption of literature is that the person creating it and the person consuming it have similar brain structures.

Main Idea: The subtle evolution of the brain over time has lead to a similar change in the kind of literature produced and how it function in the culture, and the assumption is that the creator and consumer of literature have similar brain structures.

1. C is correct. The fifth paragraph starts by saying "these differences", by which the author is referring to the differences in brain structure that were discussed in the previous paragraph. Remember to always put the question or quote in context.

2. B is correct. The author makes a point of saying that in modern society literature is a distraction from the environment and that the entertainment value crowds out other possible meanings. That best fits choice B.

3. A is correct. The author is only concerned with a central contrast between how the literature of two different types of peoples relate to the differences in their brains. It's entirely possible that there are other differences that relate to other functions, but the author doesn't care to discuss them. The prefrontal cortex may be involved with slow, careful judgment in different contexts that pure reading.

4. A is correct. The author is discussing the evolution of the brain and thus "selected for" means that the environment allowed those "selected for" to be successful in an evolutionary sense—to produce more offspring.

5. D is correct. The author's central thesis is that subtle evolutionary changes in the brain paralleled changes in the literature produced and consumed by people. If testing proved that no such evolution had happened, as choice D asserts, then the author's thesis would be disproven.

CARS Practice Passage 3

The barriers to entry into the medical field and the training of physicians creates a twofold process by which those who end up spending their lives as doctors are those who most strongly filter their experiences through the basic defense mechanism of intellectualization. They are expected to approach diseases through a rational analysis of signs, symptoms, diagnoses and prognoses, rather than the raw immediacy of sensation, intuition, feelings and family. To even apply to medical school with a realistic hope of matriculating, students must complete coursework that both demands a strong native ability to solve intellectual problems and tends to develop that intellectual capacity at the expense of other axes of human development.

Medical training = intellectual not sensation/intuiting/feeling

Most patients, on the other hand, experience both illness and wellness through the fuzzier lens of intuition, despite having health care providers who deal with them as if they were as rational as the providers themselves. Understandably, the physicians' tendency to think of diseases processes entirely through their intellect does have an effect on those patients who, by dint of their own higher education, are also predisposed to intellectualize problems. This mode of communication can partially serve to lessen the impact of bad news, but the doctor-patient relationship should do more. Regardless of how much more, it remains clear that physicians are largely ignorant of the value of processing life through intuitive, emotive processes.

Physican = rational   patient experience = intuition

This narrow vision gives precedence to rigidly informational modes of communication over the personal, emotive ones. Intentionally or not, physicians casually dismiss the possibility that a patient can only truly understand the doctor's communication in emotive terms, as they process major life events, especially traumatic ones, that way. While it is impossible to expect physicians to entirely shift the way they personally think about the matrix of pathologies that constitutes their work, we can, perhaps, ameliorate the problem by keeping what is good about intellectualization while leavening it with a dose of humanistic intuition.

physicians need to recognize & integrate some humanity/emotions

First, medical school selection criteria need to be adjusted to take account of fundamental skills of communication and empathy that most develop innately. This may be something as simple as requiring coursework outside the usual array of basic science courses expected by most medical school admissions committees. The admissions officers could also place much heavier weight on the interview, and on sample patient interactions. Finally, the interviewing process could include explicit psychological testing to assess a candidate's ability to both read and communicate emotion. *Ways to improve medical school*

Second, the training of future physicians through the medical school and residency systems must focus on identifying those physicians who excel at direct, emotive communications with patients, and help future practitioners model these behaviors. While not everyone may be trained to process illness in an emotive way, future physicians can at least learn to mimic those communication styles that will be more effective in reaching their patients. By having students practice modeling very specific behaviors and approaches to communication within the very first weeks of school, the groundwork can be laid that will have a positive impact on an entire career. *how to mimic good emotive behavior*

Finally, those physicians currently in practice ought to work, through the current system of Continuing Medical Education (CME) credits to change their communication styles. Mock-clinical interactions can take the place of the ineffectual lecture-style approach to CME credits currently so popular among practitioners. By requiring a certain number of Clinical CMEs each year, state medical boards around the country can quickly begin to change the landscape in which patients currently interact with their doctors: a landscape whose contours are solely defined by the abstract and intellectual. *change current*

1. The author makes which of the follow underlying assumptions about physicians?
   A. Only people who already filter their life experience through their intellect want to become physicians.
   B. Most of them tend to have less emotional and more intellectual personalities than the average citizen.
   C. Many of them are incapable of understanding their emotional reactions to the illness and death they confront in their work.
   D. Some of them would welcome a more rigorous set of CME requirements that include developing new styles of communication in the clinic.

2. Which of the following most accurately characterizes the author's attitude towards the communication styles most commonly employed by physicians currently?
   A. Supportive
   B. Critical
   C. Vituperative
   D. Cautious

3. The author would most likely support adding which of the following courses to the standard pre-medical curriculum?
   A. Vertebrate Immunology
   B. Critical Media Studies
   C. Psychology of Art
   D. Mathematics

4. If a medical school were to institute a policy requiring all of its faculty to participate in clinical CME courses designed to facilitate more effective communication, the author would:
   A. support the decision, as the faculty of any medical school must stay abreast of the latest developments in their respective fields.
   B. oppose the decision, because it would be a misallocation of the institution's resources and its faculty's time.
   C. support the decision, since more effective communication would require a more intuitive approach than the intellectualization their students typically learn from them.
   D. neither support nor oppose the decision, because he is primarily concerned with adjusting the process by which students are filtered before entering medical school rather than their training once there.

5. The author's main goal behind his suggestion for reform in the selection and development of future doctors is most likely:
   A. to allow patients to communicate with their doctors in a way that is comfortable for the patient and more likely to change the patients' behavior.
   B. to redress the author's own failings in his communications with his own patients.
   C. to encourage students in the arts who would otherwise not have considered medical school to bring their more direct, emotive communication styles into medicine.
   D. to push medical schools to alter their curriculum such that the intellectual rigors of the work are suborned to the more useful emotive and communicative ones.

didn't fully read

CARS Practice Passage 3

The barriers to entry into the medical field and the training of physicians creates a twofold process by which those who end up spending their lives as doctors are those who most strongly filter their experiences through the basic defense mechanism of intellectualization. They are expected to approach diseases through a rational analysis of signs, symptoms, diagnoses and prognoses, rather than the raw immediacy of sensation, intuition, feelings and family. To even apply to medical school with a realistic hope of matriculating, students must complete coursework that both demands a strong native ability to solve intellectual problems and tends to develop that intellectual capacity at the expense of other axes of human development.

Cause and effect: Getting into med school and training as a doctor ensures doctors are rational, not emotional.

Most patients, on the other hand, experience both illness and wellness through the fuzzier lens of intuition, despite having health care providers who deal with them as if they were as rational as the providers themselves. Understandably, the physicians' tendency to think of diseases processes entirely through their intellect does have an effect on those patients who, by dint of their own higher education, are also predisposed to intellectualize problems. This mode of communication can partially serve to lessen the impact of bad news, but the doctor-patient relationship should do more. Regardless of how much more, it remains clear that physicians are largely ignorant of the value of processing life through intuitive, emotive processes.

Contrast: Patients are more emotional, Doctors more intellectual

Cause and effect: Intellectualization can lessen bad news

Opinion: Author thinks doctor-patient relationship should do more, doctors are ignorant for missing out on emotion.

This narrow vision gives precedence to rigidly informational modes of communication over the personal, emotive ones. Intentionally or not, physicians casually dismiss the possibility that a patient can only truly understand the doctor's communication in emotive terms, as they process major life events, especially traumatic ones, that way. While it is impossible to expect physicians to entirely shift the way they personally think about the matrix of pathologies that constitutes their work, we can, perhaps, ameliorate the problem by keeping what is good about intellectualization while leavening it with a dose of humanistic intuition.

Cause and effect: Doctors narrow view leads to communication that focuses on information

Contrast: Doctors communicate information, but patients understand emotion.

Opinion: Author thinks we can't completely fix problem, but we can make it better.

First, medical school selection criteria need to be adjusted to take account of fundamental skills of communication and empathy that most develop innately. This may be something as simple as requiring coursework outside the usual array of basic science courses expected by most medical school admissions committees. The admissions officers could also place much heavier weight on the interview, and on sample patient interactions. Finally, the interviewing process could include explicit psychological testing to assess a candidate's ability to both read and communicate emotion.

Opinion: Author thinks the criteria to get into med school should focus on emotion and empathy, offers suggestions

Second, the training of future physicians through the medical school and residency systems must focus on identifying those physicians who excel at direct, emotive communications with patients, and help future practitioners model these behaviors. While not everyone may be trained to process illness in an emotive way, future physicians can at least learn to mimic those communication styles that will be more effective in reaching their patients. By having students practice modeling very specific behaviors and approaches to communication within the very first weeks of school, the groundwork can be laid that will have a positive impact on an entire career.

Opinion: Author thinks med schools and residencies should actively teach doctors to mimic communication styles that will match patients' emotional understanding.

Finally, those physicians currently in practice ought to work, through the current system of Continuing Medical Education (CME) credits to change their communication styles. Mock-clinical interactions can take the place of the ineffectual lecture-style approach to CME credits currently so popular among practitioners. By requiring a certain number of Clinical CMEs each year, state medical boards around the country can quickly begin to change the landscape in which patients currently interact with their doctors: a landscape whose contours are solely defined by the abstract and intellectual.

Key terms: Continuing Medical Education

Cause and effect: State medical boards could change physician behavior by requiring clinical CME's based on communication style.

Main Idea: Doctors are disconnected from patients because they take an informational, rational approach to diseases and to communication whereas patients are emotional and intuitive, thus med schools, residency programs, and state medical boards should take steps to fix this.

1. B is correct. The question asks us to fit with the author's point of view about physicians. Although the question uses the word "assumption" we must still make sure the question sticks closely to the author's main idea. Only choice B fits the bill—doctors being more intellectual and less emotional was the author's main point.
   A, C: These choices are too extreme. A's "only" and C's "incapable" go beyond what the author asserts.
   D. While some doctors might be in favor of clinical CME's we're never given any information about how doctors themselves view the CMEs they must attend.

2. B is correct. The author clearly states his opinion that things need to change. Thus we know he's not a fan of the current intellectual and informational way that doctors talk to their patients. Thus choices A and D are out. Critical is a good match and choice B is the right answer.
   C. Vituperative is much too strong. While the author argues strongly in favor of change he doesn't rant about the evils of informational communication styles.

3. C is correct. The question asks about the coursework future doctors go through, so we should check back in the passage. The author asserts that they should complete coursework outside the usual science classes. Given that the author focuses so much on intuition, empathy, and emotion, the best fit is choice C. A class on psychology and on expression through art would help achieve the author's goals.
   A, D: These are the classic "science and math" that make up the current coursework.
   B. A class on breaking down the messages found in TV and other media may help future doctors think about communication styles but it missed the mark with the author's focus on emotion and intuition.

4. C is correct. The author explicitly states in the final paragraph that doctors should go through CME's to help mold their communication styles into something more fitting for their patients.

   A. While the author would support this decision, his concern is less about "keeping up with developments" than it is about a very specific problem: mismatch in communication styles between doctors and patients.

   B, D: The author would strongly support such a decision and so we may eliminate these.

5. A is correct. A question about the author's main goal should stick with our main idea, and choice A does that— the author is very concerned with how doctors communicate with their patients.

   B. We don't know if the author herself is unable to communicate well with her patients.

   C, D: While the author may support this, she never suggests getting rid of (or diminishing) the rigorous intellectual training and coursework, only supplementing it.

This page left intentionally blank.

CARS Practice Passage 4

The best-known examples of metafiction appear abruptly in the 1960's as examples of a fully realized mode of ironic writing without any obvious predecessors. Metafiction is best understood a form of novel in which the author never lets the reader forget that he is reading a novel. Rather than aim for a realistic tone that permits the reader to "lose himself" in the book, meta-fiction forces the reader to contemplate the physical act of reading itself. Despite features of meta-fiction that suggest it grew out of earlier trends in Romantic literature, few critics could directly link the style to any particular predecessors. Recently, a potent reevaluation of the work *Jacques the Fatalist and his Master* by Denis Diderot, suggests that this work may bridge the gap between metafiction and earlier writing.

[handwritten: This work bridges gap from Metafiction to other writing → wasn't one before]

Jacques the Fatalist and his Master was written between 1765 and 1780, although it was not published as a full French version until 1796. At the time, the work was largely unappreciated and received, at best, lukewarm reviews in Germany and elsewhere outside Diderot's homeland. The work centers around the relationship between Jacques and his master, who is unnamed throughout the novel. The master instructs Jacques to regale him with tales of his various romantic affairs to pass the time as they travel. As Jacques speaks, he is continually interrupted by other characters, who are themselves interrupted. Halfway through the work, Diderot even introduces "The Reader" who evinces continual exasperation with the characters and pushes them to get back on track with the tale. Within this fractured structure, the characters are consistently contradictory: one chapter focuses on two best friends who constantly duel each other, dealing grave wounds in the process. Finally, the unwieldy tale includes large sections lifted entirely from the earlier novel *Tristam Shandy*.

[handwritten: traveling, interruptions, puts reader character in, excerpt from other book]

The structure of *Jacques* helps demonstrate why metafiction developed the traits that it did. Metafiction's goal is to keep the reader focused on the act of reading itself. It does this by eschewing the usual linear narrative structure. If the reader's expectations are wholly thwarted, he is put in a state of "high alert" that does not permit him to lose himself in the book. Metafiction also plays with the typography and physical layout of the words on the page. By continually shifting the typeface, or laying the words in groups or orientations other than a typical paragraph, the reader's attention is focused on the level of the words on the page itself rather than on the meaning behind those words. Finally, metafiction shifts narrative voice, making use of the second person (e.g. "You open the door.") to address the reader directly.

[handwritten: reader focus on act of reading; move words, keep author on "high alert"]

In *Jacques*, we may see predecessors of many of these traits. In the earliest German translations, which predate even the first full publication in France, the book shifts from traditional paragraphs to the layout more commonly used in scripts and back again, with no seeming relationship between the layout and the content of the story itself. In addition, by including "the Reader" as a character, Diderot anticipated the use of second person by metafiction authors who came two centuries later.

But ultimately it may be the breaking of narrative structure which reveals the most about how and why metafiction developed. As early as the late 1700's, critics spoke of literature as a "dying art". It was believed that everything that could be said had been said. "After [H]omer and Shakespeare," one critic opined, "what [is] left for us to say?" Much of the artistic fervor on the Continent during the time was found in the theater, and it is believed that authors sought to capture the immediacy of live plays, most notably the theater of the absurd. The wild shifts in the narrative of these plays were seen to have great comedic effect, and we can now see that *Jacques* sought to capture that energy and humor. In that regard, we may draw a straight line directly from *Jacques* to the 1960's, in which writers sought to use metafiction to capture the energy of the counter-cultural movement and its chosen form of self-expression: rock and roll music.

[handwritten: authors tried to revive boring literature → make it like plays → change narrative structure]

1. Why does the author include a discussion of literary critics who felt that literature was a dying art?
    A. To indicate how old the notion is that "everything that could be said ha[s] been said"
    B. To illustrate why metafiction sought to address the reader directly in the second person narrative voice
    C. To argue that the metafiction of the 1960's bears a direct relationship with *Jacques*
    D. To demonstrate that critics are often wrong when they make assessments that bear on the future of an art

2. If it were later discovered that in Diderot's original manuscript of *Jacques* that he included several sections of dialogue written upside down, this would:
    A. demonstrate the sloppiness with which printers approached their art in the 18th century.
    B. further support the author's thesis by provided a link between *Jacques* and later metafiction.
    C. provide a concrete reason why the work was poorly received.
    D. weaken the author's contention that *Jacques* contained features that focused the reader on the physical act of reading.

3. The passage provides information to answer all of the following questions EXCEPT:
    A. What feature of metafiction made the reader focus on the physical act of reading?
    B. The relationship between *Jacques* and the theater of the time is most closely analogous to the relationship between the meta-fiction of the 1960's and what art?
    C. Did any writers from the 1960's other than writers of metafiction make use of the second person?
    D. Does metafiction have any features that it shares with earlier Romantic fiction?

4. Which of the following, if discovered, would most *weaken* the author's thesis?
    A. No meta-fiction writers from the 1960's had read, or were even aware of *Jacques*.
    B. Even readers who are reading a traditional narrative maintain some level of attention on the physical act of reading.
    C. Diderot was unaware of developments in arts outside literature.
    D. It was common in the 18th century for novelists to quote entire passages from earlier works.

5. Literary analysts may find themselves discussing the subjects of their inquiry in a less than objective way. Which of the following would the author of this passage most likely have written?
    A. *Tristam Shandy*, by contrast, is a masterful construct that rewards both the casual reader and the most focused literary analyst.
    B. *Jacques* is a trifle of a book, with a quick breezy air that belies its philosophical heft.
    C. Metafiction leaves us feeling like we have read the ultimate expression of the writer's art; we have scaled the intellectual Mount Olympus of writing and come down again the other side, changed, but not perhaps for the better.
    D. Not an easy work to read, *Jacques* goes down less like a smooth glass of wine and more like a sharp medicine that fights you every step of the way.

CARS Practice Passage 4

The best-known examples of metafiction appear abruptly in the 1960's as examples of a fully realized mode of ironic writing without any obvious predecessors. Metafiction is best understood a form of novel in which the author never lets the reader forget that he is reading a novel. Rather than aim for a realistic tone that permits the reader to "lose himself" in the book, meta-fiction forces the reader to contemplate the physical act of reading itself. Despite features of meta-fiction that suggest it grew out of earlier trends in Romantic literature, few critics could directly link the style to any particular predecessors. Recently, a potent reevaluation of the work Jacques the Fatalist and his Master by Denis Diderot, suggests that this work may bridge the gap between metafiction and earlier writing.

Key terms: metafiction, Jacques the Fatalist, Denis Diderot

Opinion: Jacques may help link metafiction to earlier literary traditions

Cause and effect: metafiction pushes the reader to think about the physical act of reading

Jacques the Fatalist and his Master was written between 1765 and 1780, although it was not published as a full French version until 1796. At the time, the work was largely unappreciated and received, at best, lukewarm reviews in Germany and elsewhere outside Diderot's homeland. The work centers around the relationship between Jacques and his master, who is unnamed throughout the novel. The master instructs Jacques to regale him with tales of his various romantic affairs to pass the time as they travel. As Jacques speaks, he is continually interrupted by other characters, who are themselves interrupted. Halfway through the work, Diderot even introduces "The Reader" who evinces continual exasperation with the characters and pushes them to get back on track with the tale. Within this fractured structure, the characters are consistently contradictory: one chapter focuses on two best friends who constantly duel each other, dealing grave wounds in the process. Finally, the unwieldy tale includes large sections lifted entirely from the earlier novel *Tristam Shandy*.

Key terms: The Reader

Opinion: Author doesn't seem to like the book very much—calls it fractured, unwieldy, lukewarm; critics at the time didn't like it either.

The structure of Jacques helps demonstrate why metafiction developed the traits that it did. Metafiction's goal is to keep the reader focused on the act of reading itself. It does this by eschewing the usual linear narrative structure. If the reader's expectations are wholly thwarted, he is put in a state of "high alert" that does not permit him to lose himself in the book. Metafiction also plays with the typography and physical layout of the words on the page. By continually shifting the typeface, or laying the words in groups or orientations other than a typical paragraph, the reader's attention is focused on the level of the words on the page itself rather than on the meaning behind those words. Finally, metafiction shifts narrative voice, making use of the second person (e.g. "You open the door.") to address the reader directly.

Key terms: structure, typeface

Cause and effect: shifting layout, typeface, voice lets metafiction works keep the reader on their toes and focused on the act of reading itself

In Jacques, we may see predecessors of many of these traits. In the earliest German translations, which predate even the first full publication in France, the book shifts from traditional paragraphs to the layout more commonly used in scripts and back again, with no seeming relationship between the layout and the content of the story itself. In addition, by including "the Reader" as a character, Diderot anticipated the use of second person by metafiction authors who came two centuries later.

Opinion: Author sees connection between Jacques and metafiction

But ultimately it may be the breaking of narrative structure which reveals the most about how and why metafiction developed. As early as the late 1700's, critics spoke of literature as a "dying art". It was believed that everything that could be said had been said. "After [H]omer and Shakespeare," one critic opined, "what [is] left for us to say?" Much of the artistic fervor on the Continent during the time was found in the theater, and it is believed that authors sought to capture the immediacy of live plays, most notably the theater of the absurd. The wild shifts in the narrative of these plays were seen to have great comedic effect, and we can now see that Jacques sought to capture that energy and humor. In that regard, we may draw a straight line directly from *Jacques* to the 1960's, in which writers sought to use metafiction to capture the energy of the counter-cultural movement and its chosen form of self-expression: rock and roll music.

Cause and effect: Jacques and metafiction used similar techniques to capture the energy of another art form—theater for Jacques and rock music for metafiction.

Main Idea: Despite seeming like it came out of nowhere, metafiction does have connections to earlier literature, most notably Jacques. Both used similar techniques in an effort to capture the energy of another art form into their literature.

1. C is correct. The critics mentioned in the question are discussed in the final paragraph. In that paragraph we see the author's central thesis: that *Jacques*'s relationship to theater is a predecessor and analogue to metafiction's relationship to rock and roll music.
   A. The idea that there's nothing new under the sun certainly is an old idea, but the age of that cliché doesn't bear on the author's thesis in the final paragraph.
   B. We're told that using the second voice was done in order to keep the reader on their toes and this is discussed in paragraph three, not the final paragraph.
   D. While critics may often be wrong, quoting a single example doesn't prove that they're often wrong, nor does the author try to make that point.

2. B is correct. Having text printed upside down would force the reader to turn the book around. This would be the kind of technique metafiction would use to force the reader to remain focused on the physical act of reading itself. That *Jacques* did such a thing strengthens the author's thesis about the connection between *Jacques* and later metafiction.
   A. This is out of scope. The technology for printing books is never discussed.
   C. We don't know if readers of the time would have found upside down printing amusing, interesting, or wholly negative.
   D. This is the opposite of what the question says. Having to turn the book upside down would force you be aware of the physical act of reading a book.

3. C is correct. The author doesn't discuss other writers from the 1960's and thus the passage contains no information to answer the question in choice C.
   A. This question is answered in ¶3.
   B. This question is answered in the final paragraph.
   D. This is answered in ¶1.

4. C is correct. As our main idea tells us, the author's thesis is that there is a link between metafiction and earlier literature in *Jacques* because both attempted to capture the energy of another art form in their literature. If choice C is true, then Diderot could not have possibly been trying to capture the energy of the "theater of the absurd" since he would have been unaware of it.

    A. The author isn't attempting to argue that metafiction writers themselves were directly trying to imitate *Jacques* but rather that there was a literary tradition preceding metafiction that included some of its elements.

    B. That metafiction focused almost entirely on the physical act of reading doesn't mean other readers aren't somewhat aware of the act of reading.

    D. The fact that *Jacques* quotes from an earlier work is a random supporting detail not directly related to the author's thesis.

5. D is correct. This question asks us to take the author's general discussion and see which answer choices uses subjective language while still staying within the author's views. He describes *Jacques* as fractured, contradictory, and unpopular. Those words suggest choice D—that *Jacques* is not an easy work to read.

    A. We don't see anything in the passage that lets us infer the author's opinion of *Tristam Shandy*.

    B. "Quick" and "breezy" don't fit the word choice the author used is describing *Jacques*.

    C. "Ultimate" is too strong for what the author has given us.

This page left intentionally blank.

CARS Practice Passage 5

It is not in the Indian experience to seriously consider limits on family size. Yet as early as the 1960's, the exploding Indian population began to surface as a problem, discussed first only in the rarefied atmosphere of a few Indian universities, but eventually in the halls of governmental power. The population control movement made itself felt in a number of ways: the One Child Tax Credit, the subsidization of medical care for women willing to be sterilized, and the encouragement of smaller family size through a number of other economic and cultural approaches.

government involvement in Indian family size

The major driving force behind the population control movement was a simple concern about food. Government officials tracking the nation's agricultural production had estimated that India's ability to produce enough food to feed its people would be outstripped by the growing population by 1980. Given that the world markets for staple foods was experiencing unprecedentedly high prices through the 1960's, policymakers were understandably concerned. By 1964, Indian production of rice had peaked, and most regions were starting to see declines in production as soil fertility declined.

food   ↑people catch up w/ food   soil fertility dying ↓food

Attempts to address the overpopulation issue generally fell into two broad categories: economic and cultural. The usual economic approach was to either offer tax credits to married couples who choose to have no children or one child or to levy large increases in taxes on those couples choosing to have more than one. This latter approach was taken, to dramatic effect, by China in the 1970's. Fortunately for the citizens of India, their government did not follow the draconian "One Child Policy" seen in China. Cultural approaches, on the other hand, involve government subsidy of the production of works intended to emphasize the benefits of having fewer children. Such works included direct publication of informational pamphlets (much like "public service announcements" seen on American TV) distributed to doctors' offices and, more indirectly, subsidization of movies and television programs featuring protagonists whose decision to have a small family is presented in a sympathetic light.

2 approaches to fix   directly economic (tax)   culture, subtle influence

At the extreme end of the scale, governments have attempted to control the population through direct medical intervention. Ironically, the greatest practitioner of this approach was the United States. Despite never having an overpopulation problems akin to China or India, both federal and state governments in the U.S. had several policies in the beginning of the 20th century that either encouraged or forced sterilization upon certain people. Almost uniformly, those people were racial minorities, those with psychological problems, or those who encountered the criminal justice system. Such practices were almost entirely halted by the middle of the century, but a few vestiges remain even today.

US has had most medical interventions

Despite the expenditure of tremendous amounts of time and money to address the issue, the government's concerns about overpopulation in India were eventually rendered moot. The Green Revolution came late to India, but it eventually came. The combination of plant recombination, carefully planned irrigation, and pesticide use allowed grain production worldwide to skyrocket. Beginning in Mexico in 1948, under the direction of Norman Borlaug, Mexican farmers found they could vastly increase their corn and wheat yields. In the mid 1960's, Borlaug brought his approach to India. By cultivating a particular strain of dwarf rice, Indian farmers found they were able to grow plants that could sustain much higher yields than previously possible. By 1970, the rice output of a single acre of land had doubled, and presently is over triple that ever achieved prior to 1960. By the end of the century, India became the world's most successful rice producer, and exports tons of excess food annually. The Green Revolution is often credited with having saved over a billion people from starving to death, and the greatest portion of that impact was felt in India.

found higher yield crops (mexico)
green revolution saved from starving
india esp.

1. The author would most likely *disagree* with which of the following assertions?
   A. In large part, the effectiveness of India's efforts to curb overpopulation were irrelevant.
   B. The path to population control taken by India's government was more beneficent than was that taken by China's government.
   C. The Green Revolution brought about an increase in food production that outstripped the food needs of India's exploding population.
   D. The Indian government worked both directly and indirectly to curb the Indian population beginning in the first half of the twentieth century.

2. Which of the following government policies would the author most strongly endorse?
   A. favoring economic approaches over cultural approaches to encouraging smaller family size
   B. linking federal welfare dollars for unwed mothers to a requirement to submit to sterilization
   C. creating federally-owned movie studios to produce films with protagonists with only one child
   D. subsidies for the further development of crop strains that can increase yield per acre

3. An Indian government official who advocates economic incentives to small family size would likely endorse which of the following?
   I. tax credits to married couples choose to have one child or no children
   II. a negative income tax for adults choosing to remain unmarried and childless
   III. a graduated taxation scale in which families pay taxes that increase slightly with each additional child born
   A. I only
   B. I and II only   → china's approach
   C. I and III only
   D. II and III only

4. The passage information most strongly supports the inference that:
   A. population controls through direct medical intervention were popular throughout Europe.
   B. the level of food production in the United States has generally been adequate for its population.
   C. the horrors of eugenics carried out in certain countries in the mid-20th century lead to the total eradication of force sterilization throughout the world.
   D. the present global average rice production per acre is more than 300% that of the average rice production per acre in the 1950's.

5. If, in the 21st century, the effects of the Green Revolution in India were to both spread to the whole globe and to have had further improvements in their effectiveness, which of the following is most likely?
   A. Increases in the average tax benefit for unmarried childless adults.
   B. Further investment in new genetic engineering technologies to alter crops to be more pest resistant.
   C. Governments would finally end population controls through direct medical intervention.
   D. Government subsidies for cultural works encouraging a small family would decrease or disappear.

6. Suppose that, over the course of a decade, changing climactic conditions lead to decreased crop productivity such that India finds itself with a looming overpopulation problem again. According to the passage information, which of the following is most likely?
   A. Changes to the tax structure at the federal level would take place. — why
   B. Given the failures of previous population control efforts, no new population control movement would surface in either academia or the government.
   C. Researchers would develop new strains of crops that would allow for a second Green Revolution.
   D. Local government agencies throughout India would be forced to import food staples from the U.S.

CARS Practice Passage 5

It is not in the Indian experience to seriously consider limits on family size. Yet as early as the 1960's, the exploding Indian population began to surface as a problem, discussed first only in the rarefied atmosphere of a few Indian universities, but eventually in the halls of governmental power. The population control movement made itself felt in a number of ways: the One Child Tax Credit, the subsidization of medical care for women willing to be sterilized, and the encouragement of smaller family size through a number of other economic and cultural approaches.

Key terms: One Child Tax Credit

Opinion: Indian society doesn't seriously consider limiting family size, but the Indian government used a tax subsidy to try to limit family size.

The major driving force behind the population control movement was a simple concern about food. Government officials tracking the nation's agricultural production had estimated that India's ability to produce enough food to feed its people would be outstripped by the growing population by 1980. Given that the world markets for staple foods was experiencing unprecedentedly high prices through the 1960's, policymakers were understandably concerned. By 1964, Indian production of rice had peaked, and most regions were starting to see declines in production as soil fertility declined.

Cause and effect: Concerns about population are fundamentally a concern about food supply. High prices in food markets had people concerned.

Attempts to address the overpopulation issue generally fell into two broad categories: economic and cultural. The usual economic approach was to either offer tax credits to married couples who choose to have no children or one child or to levy large increases in taxes on those couples choosing to have more than one. This latter approach was taken, to dramatic effect, by China in the 1970's. Fortunately for the citizens of India, their government did not follow the draconian "One Child Policy" seen in China. Cultural approaches, on the other hand, involve government subsidy of the production of works intended to emphasize the benefits of having fewer children. Such works included direct publication of informational pamphlets (much like "public service announcements" seen on American TV) distributed to doctors' offices and, more indirectly, subsidization of movies and television programs featuring protagonists whose decision to have a small family is presented in a sympathetic light.

Key terms: public service announcements

Contrast: China punished people for having more than one child but India rewarded people for only having one child.

Opinion: Author thinks the India approach is much better. Indian government thought it was a good idea to sponsor TV programs showing people only having one child.

At the extreme end of the scale, governments have attempted to control the population through direct medical intervention. Ironically, the greatest practitioner of this approach was the United States. Despite never having an overpopulation problems akin to China or India, both federal and state governments in the U.S. had several policies in the beginning of the 20th century that either encouraged or forced sterilization upon certain people. Almost uniformly, those people were racial minorities, those with psychological problems, or those who encountered the criminal justice system. Such practices were almost entirely halted by the middle of the century, but a few vestiges remain even today.

Opinion: Those in the US thought it was a good idea to force or coerce sterilization. Author thinks this was extreme (and ironic since the US didn't have an overpopulation problem).

Cause and effect: Force sterilization was most often done to minorities, criminals, and people with mental health issues.

Despite the expenditure of tremendous amounts of time and money to address the issue, the government's concerns about overpopulation in India were eventually rendered moot. The Green Revolution came late to India, but it eventually came. The combination of plant recombination, carefully planned irrigation, and pesticide use allowed grain production worldwide to skyrocket. Beginning in Mexico in 1948, under the direction of Norman Borlaug, Mexican farmers found they could vastly increase their corn and wheat yields. In the mid 1960's, Borlaug brought his approach to India. By cultivating a particular strain of dwarf rice, Indian farmers found they were able to grow plants that could sustain much higher yields than previously possible. By 1970, the rice output of a single acre of land had doubled, and presently is over triple that ever achieved prior to 1960. By the end of the century, India became the world's most successful rice producer, and exports tons of excess food annually. The Green Revolution is often credited with having saved over a billion people from starving to death, and the greatest portion of that impact was felt in India.

Key terms: Green Revolution, Mexico, Norman Borlaug, dwarf rice

Cause and effect: Using dwarf plants, pesticides, and irrigation the green revolution vastly increased food yields. Eventually lead to India being a rice exporter.

Main Idea: Population control fundamentally stems from a concern over food supply, and can take the form of monetary rewards, monetary punishments, or forced sterilization, but by far the preferred choice is monetary rewards. Population control was eventually rendered moot by the Green Revolution.

1. D is correct. The author asserts in the final paragraph that the population control efforts were rendered moot by the Green Revolution. That's choice A. The author calls China's policies draconian and says that the Indians were fortunate that their government didn't take that approach (choice B). The author also says in the final paragraph that India now exports food, meaning their increases in food production were greater than their population increase, so he would agree with choice C. That leaves choice D as the correct answer.

2. D is correct. The author ends the passage by telling us that concerns over a population too large for the available food supply were eventually rendered moot by the Green Revolution. Thus further increases in yield per acre would help allay any future fears about overpopulation, and the author would likely support them.

3. B is correct. The passage tells us that India took an approach of rewarding people who choose not to have more than one child, rather than punish those with more children. Thus I and II fit India's approach and choice B is correct. III would fit the approach China took.

4. B is correct. We're told that the population control efforts in the US were ironic because it never had an overpopulation problem the way other countries did. Since "overpopulation" means overpopulation relative to food production, we can infer that the US has always been able to produce enough food to feed itself and therefore choice B is correct.

5. D is correct. With a further spread and increased success of the Green Revolution, we can imagine that governments would no longer fear overpopulation, since they would have enough food to feed everyone. If that were the case, there would be no need to subsidize any cultural intervention to encourage people to have fewer children.

6. A is correct. If overpopulation re-emerged as a problem, the most likely consequence would be government officials trying once again to address the problem the same way they did last time.

3. Must-Knows

> Answering CARS questions doesn't require a complex method or splitting the questions into a huge number of different categories. Instead, you must keep a laser-sharp focus on the passage itself and answering *exactly what the question asked*.

- Instead of a method, think of the approach to the questions as a rhythm—you read, rephrase, research, and respond.
- Read: read the *exact* text of the question.
- Rephrase: understand the question by rephrasing it in your own terms.
- Research: Use your notes, your highlighting, or re-reading portions of the passage to find the relevant information.
- Respond: Either predict the answer and find the best match, or use process of elimination to find the choice that best fits your research.

Approaching Science Passages

0. Introduction

The amount of information in MCAT science passages can be truly overwhelming. You're confronted with an array of tables, figures, and text, all of which are selected from primary research journal articles. Add to all of that the time pressure of having to deal with the passage *and* its questions in only eight minutes, and you've got a recipe for getting overwhelmed.

The key is try out a number of different approaches and find one that works for you. Earlier we discussed three main approaches to dealing with CARS passages: note-taking, highlighting, and skimming. These same approaches are used in science passages, with a slight change in focus. We will briefly discuss how that focus changes, and then get right to the practice passages.

1. Three Ways to Approach Science Passages

Just as in the CARS section, you can approach the passages in a number of ways. You can go slowly and take notes, move at a moderate pace and use the highlighter, or just skim the passage quickly. Each approach has its pros and cons and you've got to try them all to see what works best for you.

Note-taking: Typically this involves spending around 4-5 minutes on the passage and then 3-4 minutes on the questions. This is somewhat risky, as some questions can be really hard or time-consuming, and by using up a bunch of the clock on the passage itself, you risk shortchanging your work on the questions.

> **MCAT STRATEGY > > >**
>
> There's no "right way" to approach science passages on the MCAT. There's only *your* right way. Be sure to practice until you've found your best approach.

When you do note-taking, you will focus on the same four categories as in CARS: key terms, cause and effect, contrast, and opinion. You will see in the explanations that follow, we use those same categories to analyze the passage. The major difference between CARS and science passages is that the science passages almost never have opinions, and have fewer contrasts. Instead, your note-taking will focus very heavily on cause and effect relationships.

Highlighting: Using the on-screen highlighter to capture key terms is faster than note-taking, but presents a real risk in science passages: over-highlighting. The temptation is to highlight every acronym, technical term, and experimental step. It will take practice to find the right balance of how much highlighting to do.

One way to practice not over-highlighting is to place a hard limit on yourself: "I can only highlight three words in each paragraph." While this is too artificial to use on Test Day, it can help keep you focused on using the on-screen highlighter as a scalpel rather than a paint roller.

Skimming: Spending only 30-60 seconds on the passage itself can be very successful in the science sections, in a way that it typically isn't for CARS. However, spending less than a minute on the passage means you'll be spending tons of time looking stuff up, and more importantly you'll be relying *very* heavily on your outside knowledge.

2. Practice Passages

What follows are five practice passages taken from the various sciences. For the first passage, try a careful note-taking approach. After that, try only using a highlighter. For the third passage, try just skimming the passage. Finally, use the fourth and fifth passages to practice your preferred technique.

In the explanations that accompany each passage, you will see we've highlighted certain terms to offer an example of how you may have chosen to do your passage highlighting. This is not meant to be the "right" highlighting, since you will need to find what works best for you. We have also included notes between each paragraph. These notes focus on the Key terms, Cause and effect, Contrast, and Opinion as discussed in the CARS section of the book. These notes tend to be much more extensive that what you would actually jot down if you were doing note-taking, but again they serve as a guide for the sorts of things that are worth paying attention to.

This page left intentionally blank.

Practice Passage

Researchers investigating cognitive dissonance asked 550 adults to rate their beliefs about eating meat on a 1-5 Likert scale. On this survey, 5 is "it is healthy and ethical"; 4 is "it is somewhat healthy and ethical"; 3 is "it is neither healthy nor unhealthy and neither ethical nor unethical"; 2 is "it is somewhat unhealthy and unethical"; 1 is "it is very unhealthy and unethical."

Participants were randomly assigned to five groups:

Group 1 participants wrote an essay defending veganism and were paid $10
Group 2 participants wrote an essay defending veganism and were paid $300
Group 3 participants wrote an essay defending meat consumption and were paid $10
Group 4 participants wrote an essay defending meat consumption and were paid $300
Group 5 participants were not asked to write any essay and were not paid

After two days, participants returned to the lab and completed the attitude survey again. Table 1 shows the mean group attitude ratings.

Table 1. Effect of Essay-writing Exercise on Participant Beliefs

INITIAL ATTITUDE	GROUP 1	GROUP 2	GROUP 3	GROUP 4	GROUP 5
5 (meat okay)	4.41	4.80	4.95	4.96	4.90
4	3.30	3.75	4.11	4.08	4.01
3	2.61	2.90	3.32	3.20	3.05
2	1.61	1.95	2.38	2.15	2.11
1 (meat not okay)	1.10	1.05	1.19	1.10	1.10

In a separate experiment, researchers placed five-year old children in a room with a number of toys, including one particularly popular toy. Group 1 was given no instructions about what to play with. Group 2 was told they could play with any toy but the popular one, and that they would be mildly punished if they disobeyed. Group 3 was told they would be severely punished if they played with the popular toy. After leaving each group alone for 10 minutes, the researchers returned and told the children they could play with any toy they liked.

Analysis showed that 80% of children in Group 1 selected the popular toy. In Group 2, only 30% of children chose to play with the popular toy, even after they were permitted to. In Group 3, 68% of children elected to play with the popular toy after they were told they were allowed to.

1. Which of the following identifies a weakness in the experimental design of the first experiment?
   A. The amounts of money chosen do not reflect a constant marginal gain in value, given the differences in socioeconomic status among participants.
   B. Participants were asked to self-report their attitudes about meat consumption rather than an objective assessment.
   C. A five-point scale is too crude to make determinations about an issue as nuanced as food ethics.
   D. Both surveys conflate two factors that may be different and have different effects on cognitive dissonance.

2. The participants in the second experiment differ from those in the first in that:

    A. they did not experience cognitive dissonance.
    B. their moral reasoning likely operated on a pre-conventional level.
    C. they did experience cognitive dissonance.
    D. their cognitive development was limited to the sensorimotor stage.

3. The results from Experiment 1 most strongly suggest that those in Group 3 who initially responded with a 1, 2, or 3 on the survey:
    A. experienced increased cognitive dissonance after the second survey.
    B. resolved their cognitive dissonance by increasing certain behaviors.
    C. resolved their cognitive dissonance by changing their attitudes.
    D. decreased their ethical behavior after the essay writing task.

4. Which of the following is LEAST likely to help resolve cognitive dissonance?
    A. Changing one's behaviors
    B. Adding new cognitions
    C. Projection of dissonant attitudes
    D. Denial of the truth of the conflicting information

5. The results from Experiment 1 suggest that those in Group 2 who responded with a 3, 4, or 5 on the initial survey experienced which of the following?
    A. Less cognitive dissonance than those in Group 1 due to external justification of behavior
    B. No cognitive dissonance because they were writing an essay that was consonant or irrelevant to their attitude
    C. More cognitive dissonance than those in Group 1 due to their willingness to write an essay opposing their views in exchange for a large sum of money
    D. An increased willingness to not be truthful with the researchers

Practice Passage Explanations

Researchers investigating cognitive dissonance asked 550 adults to rate their beliefs about eating meat on a 1-5 Likert scale. On this survey, 5 is "it is healthy and ethical"; 4 is "it is somewhat healthy and ethical"; 3 is "it is neither healthy nor unhealthy and neither ethical nor unethical"; 2 is "it is somewhat unhealthy and unethical"; 1 is "it is very unhealthy and unethical."

Key term: cognitive dissonance, Likert scale, healthy, ethical

Participants were randomly assigned to five groups:

Group 1 participants wrote an essay defending veganism and were paid $10
Group 2 participants wrote an essay defending veganism and were paid $300
Group 3 participants wrote an essay defending meat consumption and were paid $10
Group 4 participants wrote an essay defending meat consumption and were paid $300
Group 5 participants were not asked to write any essay and were not paid

After two days, participants returned to the lab and completed the attitude survey again. Table 1 shows the mean group attitude ratings.

Table 1. Effect of Essay-writing Exercise on Participant Beliefs

Initial Attitude	Group 1	Group 2	Group 3	Group 4	Group 5
5 (meat okay)	4.4	4.8	4.95	4.96	4.9
4	3.3	3.75	4.1	4.08	4.01
3	2.6	2.9	3.32	3.2	3.05
2	1.6	1.95	2.38	2.15	2.11
1 (meat not okay)	1.1	1.05	1.19	1.1	1.1

Table 1 shows that attitudes in groups 1/3 ($10) had a bigger shift in response to writing their essays; biggest impact was on those positive on meat-eating who were paid $10 to defend veganism

In a separate experiment, researchers placed five-year old children in a room with a number of toys, including one particularly popular toy. Group 1 was given no instructions about what to play with. Group 2 was told they could play with any toy but the popular one, and that they would be mildly punished if they disobeyed. Group 3 was told they would be severely punished if they played with the popular toy. After leaving each group alone for 10 minutes, the researchers returned and told the children they could play with any toy they liked.

Key terms: children, toys, punishment

Contrast: 1 = play with any toy, 2 = mild punish if they use the popular toy, 3 = severe punish if they use the toy

Analysis showed that 80% of Group 1 selected the popular toy. In Group 2, only 30% of children chose to play with the popular toy, even after they were permitted to. In Group 3, 68% of children elected to play with the popular toy after they were told they were allowed to.

Cause and effect: mild punishment was the most effective deterrent for kids choosing the popular toy

1. D is correct. The self-reporting survey used conflates whether eating meat is "healthy" and whether it is "ethical". These are two very different considerations and people may have different attitudes about those two factors. In addition, differences in those attitudes may change how they react to the essay-writing exercise.
   A. The difference between \$10 and \$300 was intended to be very different values, so asserting that they do not represent a constant gain in value is not a weakness of the experiment.
   B. Many social science protocols require self-reporting. This is a standard practice, not a weakness.
   C. An inventory that assesses basic agreement or disagreement can effectively use a five-point scale.

2. B is correct. The second experiment involved small children. In Kohlberg's stages of moral reasoning, small children tend to operate at a pre-conventional level of moral reasoning. Adults typically employ conventional or post-conventional moral reasoning.
   A. The fact that children who were not threatened with a harsh punishment chose later to not play with the popular toy suggests that the children experienced cognitive dissonance and so had to adjust their internal attitude ("well I didn't want to play with that toy anyway") so that the toy was not appealing even after the threat of punishment was removed.
   C. While they did experience cognitive dissonance, this was not a way in which they differed from the adults, who also experienced cognitive dissonance.
   D. Piaget's stages of cognitive development suggest that the sensorimotor stage is limited to 0-2 year olds.

3. C is correct. Group 3 was tasked with defending meat consumption, and those who initially answered 1, 2, or 3 did not initially express an opinion that meat eating was healthy and ethical. On the repeat survey, those numbers drifted upwards considerably, suggesting that some people resolved their cognitive dissonance ("I wrote an essay defending meat-eating for only ten bucks, but I didn't think eating meat was okay.") by changing their thoughts about whether eating meat was okay.
   A. The assessment of cognitive dissonance comes through changes in the survey results between the first and second survey. We're given no data about what happens after the second survey.
   B, D: The passage doesn't address behaviors exhibited by participants, only survey responses about attitudes.

4. C is correct. Resolving cognitive dissonance requires changing thoughts or actions to reduce the dissonance. Projection is an ego defense mechanism, rather than a method to reduce cognitive dissonance.
   A, B: One can change one's behaviors to align with ideas, or add new ideas to reduce the dissonance (e.g. "I want to be on a diet but I ate that muffin. But that's okay because it must've been a low-fat muffin.").
   D. One can choose to simply ignore the new, dissonant information (e.g. "I like this presidential candidate so this news story saying he did something I disapprove of must be wrong.")

5. A is correct. Group 2 had to write an essay defending veganism, but those who answered 3, 4, or 5 did not express a particular attitude that eating meat was wrong. Thus they likely experienced some cognitive dissonance, and we can see that they resolved this dissonance by changing their ideas—in general the data on a re-test gave lower scores than the first test. However, the change in scores was not as great as for group 1. Thus Group 2 likely experienced less cognitive dissonance. The difference is that they were paid a much larger sum of money and so could justify their essay-writing behavior to themselves rather than experience unpleasant dissonance.
   B, C: According to the data in Table 1, Group 2 did not experience more dissonance or a lack of dissonance.
   D. Nothing in the passage suggests that participants had a reason to lie or did so.

Practice Passage

Aldehydes and ketones are functional groups found in a number of biologically important molecules. The structural formulas for a few examples are shown in Figure 1. The shapes of these molecules play an important role in their function and how they interact with different types of nerve receptors. For example, carvone has two optically active forms that have distinctly different flavor sensations. R-carvone is known as oil of spearmint, whereas S-carvone is the oil of caraway seeds.

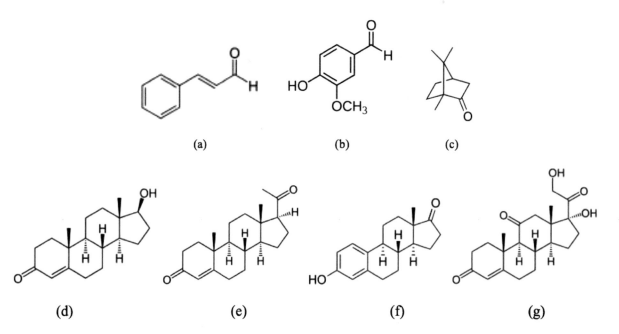

Figure 1. Structures of: (a) cinnamon; (b) vanillin; (c) camphor; (d) testosterone; (e) progestrone; (f) estrone; (g) cortisone

Both Benedict's reagent and Tollen's reagent are useful ways to test for aldehydes. In the former, a positive test results when the basic royal blue cupric solution is reduced to form a precipitate of cuprous oxide. A positive test for the latter results when the ammonia solution of silver ion is reduced to silver metal.

1. Which of the following would NOT give a positive Benedict's test?
   - I. Cinnamon
   - II. Vanillin
   - III. Camphor
   - IVs. Carvone
   - A. I and II only
   - B. I and III only
   - C. II and IV only
   - D. III and IV only

2. What are the oxidation numbers of the silver species in the Tollen's test before and after a positive test?
   - A. +1 and 0, respectively
   - B. +2 and +1, respectively
   - C. +1 and +2, respectively
   - D. +2 and 0, respectively

3. Which of the following best describes the isomer of 2-methyl-5-(1-methylethenyl)-2-cyclohexenone shown below?

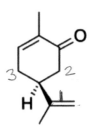

A. This isomer is R-carvone, which is oil of spearmint.
B. This isomer is R-carvone, which is oil of caraway.
C. This isomer is S-carvone, which is oil of spearmint.
D. This isomer is S-carvone, which is oil of caraway.

4. Which of the following would be most useful in distinguishing propanal from propanone?
    A. Proton NMR spectroscopy
    B. IR spectroscopy
    C. UV-Vis spectroscopy
    D. Rotation of plane-polarized light *Need to be chiral*

5. Cholesterol, whose structure is shown below, is the precursor to which of the following hormones?

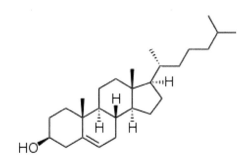

I. Testosterone
II. Estrogen
III. Cortisone
    A. I only
    B. I and II only
    C. I and III only
    D. I, II, and III
    trust yourself!

Practice Passage Explanations

Aldehydes and ketones are functional groups found in a number of biologically important molecules. The structural formulas for a few examples are shown in Figure 1. The shapes of these molecules play an important role in their function and how they interact with different types of nerve receptors. For example, carvone has two optically active forms that have distinctly different flavor sensations. R-carvone is known as oil of spearmint, whereas S-carvone is the oil of caraway seeds.

Key terms: Aldehydes, ketones, carvone, spearmint, caraway

Cause and effect: the shape of the molecule can change interactions with nerve receptors; two stereoisomers of carvone have different tastes

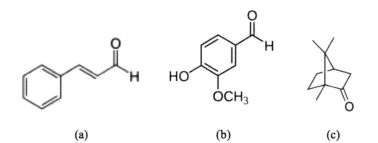

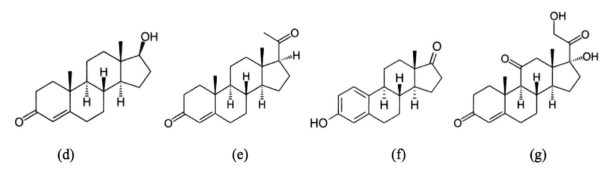

Figure 1. Structures of: (a) cinnamon; (b) vanillin; (c) camphor; (d) testosterone; (e) progestrone; (f) estrone; (g) cortisone

Figure 1 shows us the structures of various molecules with a carbonyl carbon, including both aldehydes such as cinnamon and ketones such as testosterone

Both Benedict's reagent and Tollen's reagents are useful ways to test for aldehydes. In the former, a positive test results when the basic royal blue cupric solution is reduced to form a precipitate of cuprous oxide. A positive test for the latter results when the ammonia solution of silver ion is reduced to silver metal.

Key terms: Benedict's, Tollen's

Contrast: Benedicts test involves reducing copper from cupric to cuprous solution vs. Tollen's test involves reducing a positive silver ion to silver metal

1) D is correct. As seen in the structure shown in Figure 1, the structures for cinnamon and vanillin have aldehyde functional groups, which would give a positive Benedict's test. Choices A and B can be eliminated. Also as seen in Figure 1, the structure of camphor has a ketone as a functional group. Ketones do not give a positive Benedict's test.

Choice C can be eliminated and choice D is the best answer. While the structure of carvone is not shown in Figure 1, the suffix -one, indicates that it is a ketone.

2) A is correct. As stated in the passage, Tollen's test involves the reduction of silver ion, Ag^+, to solid silver, whose oxidation number is 0. Therefore the oxidation number changes from +1 to 0.

3) D is correct. The chiral carbon of carvone in the structure shown, is at the bottom of the six membered ring. We need to assign priority to the groups attached to this carbon. The hydrogen is easily assigned the lowest priority. Since the other three positions all are directly attached to a carbon atom, we then need to turn our attention to the atoms attached to those carbons. The highest priority is assigned to the carbon that is attached to two other carbon atoms, rather than part of the ring. We now need to consider the carbons that are part of the ring. The substituent with the second highest priority is on the right side of the ring because of the ketone, followed by the carbon on the left side of the ring. With the C-H bond oriented away from the page, the remaining substituents are connected in a counterclockwise fashion in order of priority, making this the S-enantiomer. Choices A and B can be eliminated. As stated in the passage, the S-enantiomer is "oil of caraway."

4) A is correct. Propanone (acetone), has two methyl groups on either side of the carbonyl and would produce a singlet in the HNMR spectrum between 1-2 ppm. Propanal has an ethyl group and aldehyde hydrogen on either side of the carbonyl. The ethyl group will produce a triplet in the 1-2 ppm methyl region and a quartet in the 2-3 ppm methylene region. In addition, the aldehyde hydrogen will produce a singlet somewhere significantly downfield, in the 8-13 ppm range. Perhaps the easiest way to distinguish between the spectra of these molecules—and to predict that proton NMR spectroscopy would be the best way to do so—is to recognize that propanone only has one group of chemically equivalent protons (on the methyl groups), whereas propanal has three such groups.

B, C, D: Propanal and propanone are both expected to have a carbonyl stretches in the 1700-1800 cm^{-1} region of the IR spectrum and would be difficult to distinguish based on IR spectroscopy. Choice B can be eliminated. Both molecules are colorless organic compounds and would only absorb ultraviolet radiation. It would be difficult to distinguish these compounds based on UV-Vis spectroscopy. Choice C can be eliminated. Neither propanol nor propanone have chiral carbon atoms and will not rotate plane-polarized light. Choice D can be eliminated.

5) D is correct. On RN questions, our goal is to work smarter, not harder. Notice RN I is in all the answers, so do not bother checking it. The ring structure in cholesterol is similar to the ring structures in all of the steroid hormones and cholesterol is transformed by way of a series of enzymatic reactions into steroid-based sex hormones such as testosterone, progestrone and estrogen (eliminate choices A and B).

III: Cortisone is a steroid-based (i.e. cholesterol-derived) hormone produced by the adrenal gland.

Practice Passage

Figure 1 shows the dispersion of white light as it passes through a prism, resulting in seven unique beams of color. These beams can be reformed in white light if a second prism is added. Newton explained this phenomena based on the corpuscular theory of light, which describes light in terms of discrete particles that pass through matter at different speeds. Newton also recognized the ways in which light could act as a wave, in describing diffraction and interference.

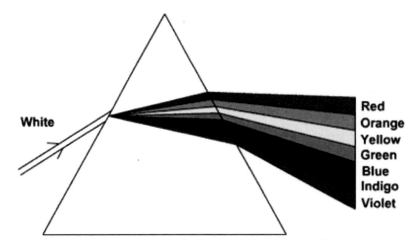

Figure 1. A schematic representation of a beam of white light passing through an equilateral triangular glass prism, resulting in the dispersion of the various color components of white light.

The angle (θ) of refraction is dependent upon the index of refraction (*n*) for a particular material, and Snell's Law (Equation 1), where *n* for a given material is a constant relating the ratio of the speed of light in a vacuum (c = 3.0 × 10^8 m/s) to the speed (v) of light in a material.

Equation 1 $n_1 \sin \theta_1 = n_2 \sin \theta_2$

The understanding of why humans see colors is based on two types of photosensitive cells, rods and cones, on the retina, located on the back of the eye, where the lens focuses light based on the principles of refraction, producing an image. The cones can be subdivided into three types (blue, green and red) based on the wavelengths of maximum sensitivity. However, each cone actually has sensitivity to a range of wavelengths.

Monochromatic light is perceived by the brain due to the degree of optic nerve stimulation that is generated by the combination of each type of photosensitive cell. Materials that reflect multiple colors produce complex responses from the cones. The most common type of color dysfunction is known as red-green color blindness, in which the red or green cones are either missing or function with diminished efficiencies. This abnormality is often associated with a recessive X chromosome mutation.   XY   XX

1. A red-green colorblind man is married to a red-green carrier woman. What are the probabilities that a male child and female child in this family will be red-green colorblind?
   A. The probability for green-red colorblindness will be 100% for the male children and 0% for the female children.
   B. The probability for green-red colorblindness will be 50% for the male children and 25% for the female children.
   C. The probability for green-red colorblindness will be 50% for the male children and 50% for the female children.
   D. The probability for green-red colorblindness will be 100% for the male children and 50% for the female children.

2. If a red laser pointer is focused on the surface of a rectangular piece of glass (n = 1.50) at an angle of 30° with respect to the normal, what would be the angle that the laser bean exits the other side of the glass?
    A. 20°
    B. 30°
    C. 45°
    D. 60°

3. Which of the following monochromatic colors has the lowest velocity while passing through a glass prism?
    A. Red
    B. Yellow
    C. Green
    D. Blue

4. Which of the following best describes a corpuscle of light?
    A. A proton
    B. An electron
    C. A neutron
    D. A photon

5. If the human eye has a converging lens, which of the following best describes the image that is formed on the retina for an object that is more than one focal length away from the lens?
    A. The image is real and inverted.
    B. The image is real and erect.
    C. The image is virtual and inverted.
    D. The image is virtual and erect.

91

Practice Passage Explanations

Figure 1 shows the dispersion of white light as it passes through a prism, resulting in seven unique beams of color. These beams can be reformed in white light if a second prism is added. Newton explained this phenomena based on the corpuscular theory of light, which describes light in terms of discrete particles that pass through matter at different speeds. Newton also recognized the ways in which light could act as a wave, in describing diffraction and interference.

Key terms: prism, refraction, diffraction, interference

Cause and effect: white light = entire visible spectrum (ROYGBIV); white light through a prism → different wavelengths have difference indices of refraction → dispersion and the separation of colors

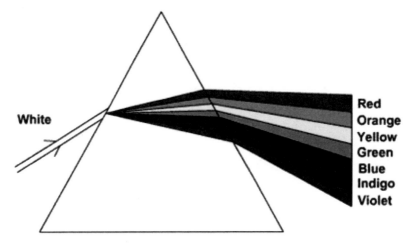

Figure 1. A schematic representation of a beam of white light passing through an equilateral triangular glass prism, resulting in the dispersion of the various color components of white light.

Figure 1 shows what happens when light rays pass from air (low n) to glass (high n), light is bent towards the normal, each colors bends to a different degree due to its inherent properties

The angle (θ) of refraction is dependent upon the index of refraction (n) for a particular material, and Snell's Law (Equation 1), where n for a given material is a constant relating the ratio of the speed of light in a vacuum ($c = 3.0 \times 10^8$ m/s) to the speed (v) of light in a material.

Equation 1 $n_1 \sin \theta_1 = n_2 \sin \theta_2$

Equation 1 shows that angle of the light (with respect to the normal line) will be inversely proportional to the index of refraction—if $n_1 > n_2$ then $\theta_1 < \theta_2$

The understanding of why humans see colors is based on two types of photosensitive cells, rods and cones, on the retina, located on the back of the eye, where the lens focuses light based on the principles of refraction, producing an image. The cones can be subdivided into three types (blue, green and red) based on the wavelengths of maximum sensitivity. However, each cone actually has sensitivity to a range of wavelengths.

Key terms: photosensitive cells, rods, cones

Cause and effect: light on photoreceptors → human vision (color); 3 types of cones (color) sensitive to different wavelengths

Monochromatic light is perceived by the brain due to the degree of optic nerve stimulation that is generated by the combination of each type of photosensitive cell. Materials that reflect multiple colors produce complex responses from the cones. The most common type of color dysfunction is known as red-green color blindness, in which the red or green cones are either missing or function with diminished efficiencies. This abnormality is often associated with a recessive X chromosome mutation.

Key terms: monochromatic light, color blindness, recessive, X chromosome

Cause and effect: mutation on the X chromosome → dysfunction of one or more cones → color blindness

1. C is correct. Since the father is color blind, he carries the mutated gene (*) on his X chromosome (X*Y) and the mother is heterozygous for the mutation (X*X). The Punnett square is:

	X*	X
X*	X*X*	X*X
Y	X*Y	XY

Since the mutated gene is recessive, 50% of the female children will be colorblind and 50% of the male children will be color blind.

2. B is correct. When the light beam goes from the air (n ≈ 1) into the glass the angle will be bent towards the normal as predicted by Snell's law.

$$1 \sin 30° = 1.50 \sin \theta_{glass}$$

$$(1/1.5) \sin 30° = \sin \theta_{glass}$$

$$(1/1.5)\ 0.5 = \sin \theta_{glass}$$

However, on the other side of the glass the beam will bend back away from the normal, therefore:

$$1.5 \sin \theta_{glass} = 1 \sin \theta_{air}$$

$$(1.5/1)\ (1/1.5)\ 0.5 = \sin \theta_{air}$$

$$0.5 = \sin \theta_{air}$$

$$\sin^{-1} (0.5) = \theta_{air}$$

$$30° = \theta_{air}$$

The light beam that exits the glass on the other side is parallel to the incident light beam, with the angle with respect to the normal being 30°.

3. D is correct. Based on Figure 1, the blue light is refracted the most. In order for this to happen the index of refraction (n) for this color must be the highest. Since $n = c/v$, where c is the speed of light in a vacuum and v is the velocity in the prism, the velocity of the blue light will be the slowest and red light will be the fastest.

4. D is correct. Choices A, B and C all correspond to components of atoms and have mass. Light does not have mass. As stated in the first paragraph of the passage, "... corpuscular theory of light, which describes light in terms of discrete particles ..." and photons are the modern term used to describe a particle of electromagnetic radiation (light).

5. A is correct. A converging lens produces a real and inverted image for objects located beyond the focal point of the lens (o >f), as shown below in the ray diagrams for a convex lens below.

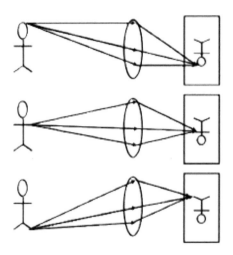

This page left intentionally blank.

Practice Passage

In Baumrind's exploration of attachment theory, she initially classified three patterns of child behaviors. Pattern I is characterized by children being secure, self-reliant, and explorative. Pattern II is when children tend to withdraw, are distrustful, and are discontent. Pattern III consists of children who have little self-control, tend to retreat from novel experiences, and lack self-reliance.

Baumrind postulated that specific parenting styles lead to children developing one of these patterns, and classified preschool children as belonging to one of the patterns based on five criteria: self-control, approach-avoidance tendency, self-reliance, subjective mood, and peer affiliation.

Children who exhibit Pattern I behavior tend to be perceived as having the "healthiest" developmental behaviors, so efforts have been made to foster this style in children. A study was conducted to assess parenting styles before and after a training intervention designed to foster Authoritative techniques, which are associated with development of Pattern 1 behavior. Two hundred couples were recruited and their parenting style was identified. Parent-child interactions were observed for 1 hour a day for 10 days, both before and after training. Figure 1 shows the approximate proportion of couples employing each parenting style.

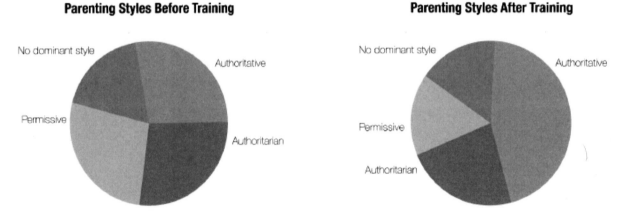

Figure 1. Results of parenting styles before and after training

Parenting behavior was considered and coded in the following areas: control, parental maturity demands, communication, and nurturance. The results showed that parents of Pattern I children were consistent with their children, respected child independence, but held the children to a position once decided, demonstrated control of the children, were supportive, and communicated clearly. This style of parenting was deemed Authoritative parenting. Parents of Pattern II children, deemed Authoritarian parents, were highly controlling of the children, provided little nurturance, did reason with the child, and did not encourage children to communicate. Finally, Pattern III children came from parents that were not controlling, were less organized, were more insecure about parenting, and tended to use withdrawal of love as a consequence for child behavior. This approach was designated Permissive parenting.

1. It can be expected that after the training children will begin to demonstrate what type of Pattern of behavior more than before the training?
   - A. Pattern I
   - B. Pattern II
   - C. Pattern III
   - D. Pattern IV

2. An infant who demonstrates Pattern I behavior and whose parents' parenting style is Authoritative probably has what type of attachment style with his parent?
   A. Anxious-Ambivalent
   B. Avoidant
   C. Disorganized
   D. Secure

3. What could be a reason for research that found that Authoritarian parenting may be a healthier parenting style in some instances?
   A. Different cultural norms
   B. Pattern II behavior is healthier
   C. Attachment style changes frequently over time
   D. Long-term outcomes aren't associated with early attachment

4. Authoritative parents are probably best able to help their child resolve what first Eriksonian developmental stage?
   A. Intimacy vs. Isolation
   B. Trust vs. Mistrust
   C. Formal operations vs. Concrete operations
   D. Oedipal vs. Latency

5. If a child does not have a secure attachment with his caregivers and later is unable to form secure attachments, he may have missed what period of time for learning to develop attachments?
   A. Attachment period
   B. Latency period
   C. Imprinting period
   D. Post-natal period

Practice Passage Explanations

In Baumrind's exploration of attachment theory, she initially classified three patterns of child behaviors. Pattern I is characterized by children being secure, self-reliant, and explorative. Pattern II is when children tend to withdraw, are distrustful, and are discontent. Pattern III consists of children who have little self-control, tend to retreat from novel experiences, and lack self-reliance.

Key terms: attachment theory, Baumrind, 3 patterns of behavior

Baumrind postulated that specific parenting styles lead to children developing one of these patterns, and classified preschool children as belonging to one of the patterns based on five criteria: self-control, approach-avoidance tendency, self-reliance, subjective mood, and peer affiliation.

Key terms: five criteria, parenting style

Opinion: Baumrind = specific parenting style → specific pattern

Children who exhibit Pattern I behavior tend to be perceived as having the "healthiest" developmental behaviors, so efforts have been made to foster this style in children. A study was conducted to assess parenting styles before and after a training intervention designed to foster Authoritative techniques, which are associated with development of Pattern 1 behavior. Two hundred couples were recruited and their parenting style was identified. Parent-child interactions were observed for 1 hour a day for 10 days, both before and after training. Figure 1 shows the approximate proportion of couples employing each parenting style.

Key terms: Pattern I behavior, Authoritative parenting

Cause and effect: Authoritative parenting → Pattern I behavior (healthiest); study sought to ↑Authoritative parenting

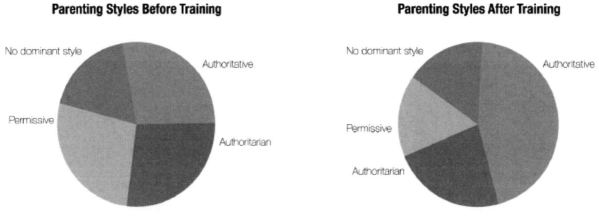

Figure 1. Results of parenting styles before and after training

Figure 1 shows us that the training leads to a significant increase in Authoritative parenting behavior, small decreases in Authoritarian and No Dominant Style and a larger decrease in Permissive parenting

Parenting behavior was considered and coded in the following areas: control, parental maturity demands, communication, and nurturance. The results showed that parents of Pattern I children were consistent with their children, respected child independence, but held the children to a position once decided, demonstrated control of the children, were supportive, and communicated clearly. This style of parenting was deemed Authoritative parenting. Parents of Pattern II children, deemed Authoritarian parents, were highly controlling of the children, provided little nurturance, did reason with the child, and did not encourage children to communicate. Finally, Pattern III children came from parents that were not controlling, were less organized, were more insecure about parenting, and tended to use withdrawal of love as a consequence for child behavior. This approach was designated Permissive parenting.

Key terms: authoritative, authoritarian, permissive parenting

Cause and effect: Authoritative → Pattern I child behavior; Authoritarian → Pattern II; Permissive → Pattern III

1. A is correct. According to the passage, Pattern I behavior is associated with Authoritative parenting style, the style of behavior that increased from before to after training.

2. D is correct. According to the passage, secure attachment style is characterized by Pattern I type behavior, which is suggested to be a result of authoritative parenting.

3. A is correct. In some cultures, having an Authoritarian parenting style may lead to healthier results for children. Particularly in unsafe environments, Authoritarian parenting has been found to keep children safer.

4. B is correct. All kids are expected to go through the stages in the same order. According to Erikson, Trust vs. Mistrust is the first stage that infants must address. Having authoritative parents helps ensure the infant is able to successfully negotiate this stage.

5. C is correct. During imprinting periods, children are sensitive for learning certain things. If this period passes and the child did not learn what he was supposed to learn, he may be unable to learn this item at a later time.

Practice Passage

Parathyroid hormone (PTH) is secreted by cells of the parathyroid glands. It acts to increase the concentration of calcium in the blood, whereas calcitonin acts to decrease calcium concentration. PTH promotes bone resorption by indirectly stimulating osteoclasts, the cells responsible for resorbing bone tissue. Osteoclasts lack PTH receptors, but PTH does bind osteoblasts—cells responsible for bone synthesis. Binding stimulates osteoblasts to increase their expression of RANKL and inhibits their expression of OPG. Binding of RANK to RANKL stimulates osteoclast differentiation. OPG binds to RANKL and blocks it from interacting with RANK. Additionally, PTH acts on the kidneys, where it enhances active reabsorption of Ca2+ and Mg2+, while decreasing reabsorption of phosphate. PTH further acts on the kidneys to increase their production of the active metabolite of Vitamin D, calcitriol, which increases the absorption of Ca2+ by the intestines.

A physician examining a 55 year old female patient complaining of abdominal pain suspected a dysfunction of calcium regulation. Laboratory analysis revealed a total serum calcium of 12.3 (normal 8.4-10.2), a serum phosphorous of 2.4 (normal 2.7-4.5), and elevated PTH. In order to make a diagnosis, the physician took the laboratory values into consideration along with the following information regarding PTH dysfunction:

Primary hyperparathyroidism can develop as a result of autonomous over-secretion of PTH by the parathyroid gland.
Secondary hyperparathyroidism is characterized by an appropriately elevated PTH response to low blood Ca2+ concentration.
Pseudohypoparathyroidism is a condition associated with resistance of cells to PTH.
An inappropriately low level of PTH in the blood due to decreased parathyroid gland function is known as hypoparathyroidism.

1. Secondary hyperparathyroidism is likely to be caused by all of the following EXCEPT:
   A. chronic kidney disease.
   B. decreased dietary calcium intake.
   C. elevated blood phosphate levels.
   D. a PTH secreting tumor.

2. Sarcoidosis, a disease involving the formation of nodules containing inflammatory cells, can lead to increased formation of calcitriol. Of the following, what is the most likely physiological effect of this disease?
   A. Decreased bone density
   B. Hypoparathyroidism
   C. Elevated urinary calcium
   D. Less intestinal calcium absorption

3. What would result from the total surgical removal of the parathyroid gland?
   A. Enhanced bone mineralization
   B. Increased cardiac contractility
   C. Neurological complications
   D. Kidney failure

4. The following findings in a symptomatic patient are most consistent with what disorder of calcium metabolism? (Note: measurement of serum Ca2+, phosphates and calcitriol concentrations and in urinary phosphorus excretion after administration of biosynthetic PTH were unchanged). Serum [PTH]: High Serum [Calcitriol]: Low Serum [Ca2+]: Low Serum [Phosphate]: High

   A. Primary hyperparathyroidism
   B. Secondary hyperparathyroidism
   C. Hypoparathyroidism
   D. Pseudohypoparathyroidism

5. Which of the following is a peptide hormone?

   A. T4
   B. Leukotrienes ← inflammatory eicosanoid
   C. Estosterone
   D. ACTH

Practice Passage Explanations

Parathyroid hormone (PTH) is secreted by cells of the parathyroid glands. It acts to increase the concentration of calcium in the blood, whereas calcitonin acts to decrease calcium concentration. PTH promotes bone resorption by indirectly stimulating osteoclasts, the cells responsible for resorbing bone tissue. Osteoclasts lack PTH receptors, but PTH does bind osteoblasts—cells responsible for bone synthesis. Binding stimulates osteoblasts to increase their expression of RANKL and inhibits their expression of OPG. Binding of RANK to RANKL stimulates osteoclast differentiation. OPG binds to RANKL and blocks it from interacting with RANK. Additionally, PTH acts on the kidneys, where it enhances active reabsorption of Ca2+ and Mg2+, while decreasing reabsorption of phosphate. PTH further acts on the kidneys to increase their production of the active metabolite of Vitamin D, calcitriol, which increases the absorption of Ca2+ by the intestines.

Key terms: parathyroid hormone (PTH), parathyroid glad, calcitonin, osteoclasts, osteoblasts, RANK, RANKL, OPG, Vitamin D, calcitriol

Contrast: PTH increases in the blood; calcitonin decreases it

Cause and effect: PTH increases calcium in blood by promoting resorption of bone; binding of RANKL by its ligand, stimulates osteoclasts; OPG binding blocks RANKL; PTH causes osteoblasts to increase RANK and inhibits OPG, thereby increasing active osteoclasts; PTH acts on the kidneys to increase Ca^{2+} and Mg^{2+} reabsorption, decrease phosphate reabsorption, and increase conversion of Vitamin D precursor to its active metabolite, calcitriol; calcitriol increases intestinal absorption of Ca^{2+}

A physician examining a 55 year old female patient complaining of abdominal pain suspected a dysfunction of calcium regulation. Laboratory analysis revealed a total serum calcium of 12.3 (normal 8.4-10.2), a serum phosphorous of 2.4 (normal 2.7-4.5), and elevated PTH. In order to make a diagnosis, the physician took the laboratory values into consideration along with the following information regarding PTH dysfunction:

Primary hyperparathyroidism can develop as a result of autonomous over-secretion of PTH by the parathyroid gland. Secondary hyperparathyroidism is characterized by an appropriately elevated PTH response to low blood Ca2+ concentration.
Pseudohypoparathyroidism is a condition associated with resistance of cells to PTH.
An inappropriately low level of PTH in the blood due to decreased parathyroid gland function is known as hypoparathyroidism.

Key terms: primary hyperthyroidism; secondary hyperthyroidism; pseudohypoparathyroidism; hypoparathyroidism

Cause and effect: the patient's lab results show elevated calcium and PTH levels; primary hyperthyroidism results from inappropriate oversecretion of PTH; secondary hyperthyroidism is an appropriately elevated PTH response to low blood calcium; hypoparathyroidism is characterized by low levels of PTH synthesis or secretion; pseudohypoparathyroidism is caused by resistance of cells to PTH

1. D is correct. Secondary hyperparathyroidism is the compensatory increase in parathyroid hormone (PTH) as a result of decreased calcium. A PTH secreting tumor would lead to an inappropriate elevation of PTH hormone and low serum calcium (high serum calcium is seen in primary hyperparathyroidism, as would result from the situation described in choice D).

A. Secondary hyperparathyroidism can be caused by chronic kidney disease, by decreasing the synthesis of calcitriol; when calcitriol levels are decreased, there is decreased calcium absorption from the GI tract, leading to decreased serum Ca2+ levels—resulting in increased PTH release

B. Secondary hyperparathyroidism can be caused by decreased dietary intake of calcium, leading to decreased serum Ca2+ levels—resulting in increased PTH release

C. Secondary hyperparathyroidism can be caused by elevated blood phosphate levels; phosphate binds Ca2+, removing free calcium from circulation, leading to decreased serum Ca2+ levels—resulting in increased PTH release

2. C is correct. Calcitriol synthesis by sarcoid granulomas will cause increased calcium absorption from the GI tract, leading to increased serum Ca2+ levels and increased urinary calcium clearance. The increase in the filtered load of Ca2+ is due to both its elevated concentration in the blood and its decreased reabsorption in the tubules secondary to an appropriate decrease in PTH secretion by the parathyroid gland.

A. An appropriate PTH response should not have a negative effect on bone mineralization.

B. The passage indicates that hypoparathyroidism is due to some dysfunction of PTH secretion, most often as a consequence of surgical removal of the thyroid or parathyroid gland, or an inherited or immune-related condition; while PTH levels would be decreased in the situation described in the question stem, it would constitute an appropriate response to changes in circulating calcium levels.

D. Calcitriol synthesis by sarcoid granulomas will cause increased calcium absorption from the GI tract.

3. C is correct. Extracellular calcium is required for both neurotransmitter release and is involved in the mechanism of contraction of the cells of the all muscle types. For this reason, physiological blood calcium concentrations are tightly regulated within a narrow range for proper cellular processes. Removal of the parathyroid gland—the source of PTH synthesis—would severely interfere with normal calcium homeostasis. Involuntary muscular contraction, referred to as tetany, and seizures may result from the condition.

A. Bone mineralization would not be increased by decreased PTH secretion.

B. Cardiac contractility, which depends on extracellular calcium influx as part of its mechanism of calcium-induced calcium release from the sarcoplasmic reticulum, would be decreased, rather than increased, in severe cases of depressed blood calcium.

D. While the kidneys are centrally involved in the body's various mechanisms of calcium homeostasis, their function does not depend on the maintenance of extracellular calcium

4. D is correct. Pseudohypoparathyroidism is one of several unrelated genetic condition where affected individuals show a common phenotype associated with resistance to PTH. Patients have a low serum calcium and high phosphate, because of resistance to the effects of PTH at the cellular level, but an appropriate elevation of PTH in response to low blood calcium concentrations.

A. Blood [Ca2+] would be elevated in primary hyperparathyroidism

B. Laboratory values such as those shown could also be due to secondary hyperparathyroidism; however, the fact that measurements of serum calcium, phosphates and calcitriol concentrations, as well as of urinary phosphorus excretion after administration of biosynthetic PTH were unchanged, indicates a primary insensitivity to PTH activity.

C. PTH would be low in hypoparathyroidism

5. D is correct. ACTH is a peptide hormone, comprised of amino acids.

A. T4 is a tyrosine-derived hormone. Thyroid hormones are lipid-soluble amino acid hormones and act at the level of transcription (unlike peptide hormones).

B. Leukotrienes are eicosanoid type inflammatory mediators produced in leukocytes by the oxidation of arachidonic acid.

C. Testosterone is a steroid hormone.

3. Must-Knows

> There's no such thing as a "right way" to tackle the science passages—only *your* right way.
>   - To figure out your right way, start practicing science passages right away. Use resources such as Next Step's Review books, online Full Lengths, or AAMC resources to get the practice you need.
> There are three main approaches to science passages:
>   - Note-taking involves a slower, more careful analysis of the passage and jotting down key ideas as you read. If you take this approach, you will have to move more quickly through the questions.
>   - Highlighting is a balanced approach where you spend a little less than half your time on the passage and a little more than half your time on the questions. This tends to be the most popular approach.
>   - Skimming means quickly looking over the figures and getting to the questions in under a minute. While this approach can save a bunch of time, it relies *very* heavily on an exceptionally strong science background.

Analyzing Science Questions

CHAPTER 6

0. Introduction to Science Questions

Analyzing science questions can be difficult for many students. The sciences may be more familiar to many pre-meds than the abstract verbal content but there's also *so* much material to learn. Yet the difficulty of the test is in *how* it tests the material, not necessarily *what* material it tests. However, a focused strategy can help you score more points through understanding the material on a fundamental level, as opposed to superficial memorizing.

1. Read/Rephrase/Research/Respond

The basic strategy for analyzing a science question is to follow the four-step framework: Read, Rephrase, Research, and Respond. We'll start by explaining and applying these steps to a sample question.

1. A patient with a tumor in his hypothalamus experiences a significant increase in vasopressin secretion from his posterior pituitary. Which of the following would be the most direct consequence of this disorder?
    A. Increased water concentration in the urine
    B. Increased total urine volume
    C. Decreased sodium ion concentration in plasma
    D. Increased secretion of thyroxine

This is an example of a relatively straightforward independent biology question. The first step, of course, is to simply **read** the question, but you must be asking yourself, *"**Exactly** what is the question asking me for?"* A classic sort of trap answer will be something that's the "right answer to the wrong question"—that is, it will be related to the topic of the question and will be a true fact, but not **exactly** answer the question.

After you've read and understood the question, then move on to **rephrasing** the question in your own terms— that is, be sure to understand the underlying task the question is asking. Here, you've read the phrase "most direct consequence" in the question so you might rephrase it as "increased vasopressin does what, with no intervening steps?" Questions can include extraneous information—here the bit about the tumor—and when you rephrase the question, you cut right to the heart of the issue.

Next, you **research** the relevant information. You ask yourself, *"What information is provided?"* You've got to be careful not to make any unwarranted assumptions. The MCAT is a picky test and will expect you to pay attention to the exact information provided. We're told that the patient in question has an *overexpression* of vasopressin and asks you for a likely consequence of the increased hormone level. You can do your research by looking up information in the passage, or by asking yourself, *"What outside information do I need?"* The independent questions especially will draw heavily on outside knowledge. Here, you need to be familiar with the physiological function of vasopressin. Vasopressin, also known as antidiuretic hormone, is a peptide hormone found in humans and other mammals. Its two primary functions are to retain water in the body and to constrict blood vessels. Vasopressin regulates the body's osmolarity by acting to increase water reabsorption in the collecting ducts of the kidney nephron. This results in more concentrated urine and more water present in the plasma. The increase in water in the plasma would decrease the concentration of sodium ions in the body.

Finally **respond** to the question by *evaluating the choices, either by prediction or process of elimination*. In "prediction" you simply skim quickly through the choices looking for what you already know the answer will say. That's often the case when you have a good content background in an area. If you're not exactly sure what they're looking for, don't delay—start eliminating choices.

Remember, *answer every question, even if you're not sure!*.

In this question, the answer is (C). Decreased sodium ion concentration in plasma. By its regulation of plasma osmolarity, the excess vasopressin in this patient will cause the patient to develop more concentrated urine and more water present in the plasma. The increase in water in the plasma would decrease the concentration of sodium ions in the body. Thus, the correct answer is (C).

A. This is the opposite of vasopressin's effect. A greater degree of water reabsorption would lower the levels of water in the urine, thus decreasing the concentration of water in the fluid excreted.

B. This is the opposite of the effects of vasopressin. Greater water retention by the kidney would serve to lower total urine volume, not increase it. This could be result of a tumor that *lowers* vasopressin release, which is why it is important to be sure of exactly what the question is asking.

D. This answer is another MCAT favorite, the one that comes out of left field, but may seem plausible if you're unsure of your content. Vasopressin is a hormone that exerts homeostatic regulation via its effects on the kidney, which is not directly involved in the actions of the thyroid, which maintains homeostasis of the body via temperature control. The thyroid controls metabolism through the effects of the thyroid hormone, thyroxine, which acts to raise metabolic activity in the body. Thus vasopressin is not directly linked to metabolic rate, which thyroxine controls.

Now try another similar question:

2. Which of the following is an example of disruptive selection?
   A. Females of a species choose to mate with males of the species based on the size and color of the males' tail feathers, with females preferentially mating with males that have larger and more colorful plumage.
   B. An insect is preyed upon by several different species of bird that rely on vision for hunting, such that the birds are more easily able to see, catch, and eat the larger insects.
   C. A type of trout competes with another fish species for food and in such competition, trout that are significantly larger than average are able to intimidate the other fish species away and trout that are significantly smaller than average are able to access food by stealth without confrontation.
   D. In a certain species of crocodile, females that are smaller than average are subject to predation by snakes and females that are larger than average are subject to hunting by humans.

Read the Question: an example of disruptive selection

Rephrase the Question: I will need to identify a situation that provides a clear example of the concept of disruptive selection.

Research: I will need to rely on my outside knowledge. Disruptive selection is a form of natural selection pressure in which members of a species gain an advantage by not being of the average type.

Respond: I can't predict the exact answer, so I will have to use process of elimination. Here, choice C gives us an example where especially large and especially small fish have a competitive advantage. This "disrupts" the population by leading to smaller and smaller fish and also larger and larger fish. Eventually these two types of fish may develop into entirely separate species.

    A. This is an example of sexual selection, a mode of natural selection in which some individuals out-reproduce other member of a population because they are better at securing mates.

    B. This is an example of directional selection, with smaller insects being favored. Directional selection is a mode of natural selection in which the environmental conditions favor an extreme phenotype over other phenotypes, causing the allele frequency to shift over time in the direction of the extreme phenotype.

    D. This is an example of stabilizing selection. Stabilizing selection is a type of natural selection that favors the average individuals in a population. This process selects against the extreme phenotypes and instead favors the majority of the population that is well adapted to the environment, with average member of the species being favored.

Now that we've carefully examined a couple of questions, complete the questions on the next page to practice this process. The explanations follow.

Practice Independent Questions

3. When exposed to milk contaminated with strontium, children's bodies will incorporate the strontium into their bones. The strontium tends to locate primarily in growing long bones. If examined, where would strontium most likely be found?
   A. Along the outer edges of the ala of the hips
   B. Near the sutures in skull bones
   C. Evenly distributed along the tibias
   D. The epiphyseal plates of the femurs

4. At the end of an organic chemistry reaction a student is left with the end product in a 100mL aqueous solution. She attempts to do an extraction using 25mL of acetone. Which of the following correctly characterizes the results she will see?
   A. The extraction will work given acetone's relative solubility in water.
   B. The extraction would work with acetone or any other organic solvent since organic molecules are insoluble in water.
   C. The student should instead perform a distillation, as distillation is the only method that can separate an organic solute from an aqueous solvent.
   D. The extraction will be unsuccessful since acetone is miscible in water.

5. Following a stroke, a patient loses certain motor functions leaving him unable to write with a pen. After months of rehab he slowly regains this ability. This demonstrates:
   A. the regrowth of damaged tissues.
   B. neural plasticity.
   C. central nervous system functions being taken over by the peripheral nervous system.
   D. the substitution of regrown glial cell function for neuronal cell function.

6. A soldier is exposed to a nerve gas which, when inhaled, binds irreversibly and non-competitively to acetylcholinesterase. The soldier is mostly likely to die from:
   A. tetanic contraction of the diaphragm.
   B. hypovolemic shock.
   C. gangrene.
   D. stroke.

Explanations

3. D is correct. The question states that strontium localizes to the growing portion of long bones, and long bones grow along their epiphyseal plates. There are four bone shapes in the human skeleton -- long bones, short bones, flat bones, and irregular bones. Long bones have a tubular shaft and articular surface at each end (e.g the bones of the arms and legs). Short bones have a tubular shaft and articular surfaces at each end but are much smaller compared to the long bones. The short bones include all of the small bones in the hands, the feet, and the clavicle. Flat bones are thin and have broad surfaces. The flat bones include the scapula, the ribs, and the sternum. Irregular bones are irregular in size and shape. They include the bones in the vertebral column, the carpal bones in the hands, tarsal bones in the feet, and the patella. The hips and the skull are flat bones, not long bones, so you may eliminate choices A and B. The question states that strontium localizes to the growing portion of long bones, and long bones grow along their epiphyseal plates. Thus choice D is correct.

    A. The ilium (ala) is the uppermost and largest bone of the pelvis, and is a flat bone.
    B. The skull and cranial bones are flat bones, not long bones.
    C. Very tempting, because is does mention a long bone, the tibia, also known as the shin bone. However, the longitudinal growth of long bones is a result of ossification at the epiphyseal plate.

4. D is correct. To carry out an extraction, the two liquids mixed must not be soluble in each other. They will separate out forming two layers in the test tube, and the solutes within them will spontaneously sort to the layer in which they are more soluble. Acetone, as a very polar molecule, readily dissolves in water. Thus it's impossible to do a water-acetone extraction and choice D is the correct answer.

    A. This is the exact opposite of the right answer, as described above.
    B. Many organic molecules are soluble in water, including acetone and many alcohols.
    C. There are many methods by which solutes can be separated from their solvent, not just distillation.

5. B is correct. Although parts of the brain are specialized for certain functions, when the brain is damaged some of that function can return through neural plasticity. The brain uses a new part to carry out the old function.

    A. The central nervous system does not regrow neurons.
    B. The peripheral nervous system functions to transport signals to and from the CNS and does not carry out complicated tasks like writing with a pen.
    D. The glia (e.g. Schwann cells and oligodendrocytes) are supporting cells and do not carry out nerve function themselves.

6. A is correct. Acetylcholinesterase is the enzyme in the neuromuscular junction that breaks down acetylcholine. This breakdown is necessary for a nerve to stop stimulating a muscle to contract—the enzyme allows the muscle to relax. If this poison gets to the diaphragm, it would not be allowed to relax, preventing the victim from exhaling. This would asphyxiate the person.

    B, D: Shock and stroke relate to problems with the circulatory system, rather than the neuromuscular system.
    C. Nothing in the question stem suggests the soldier would have infected tissue subject to gangrene, a potentially life-threatening condition that arises when a considerable mass of body tissue dies.

2. Passage-Based Science Questions

When answering the questions that accompany a passage, you should follow the same four-step approach of read, rephrase, research, and respond. The difference for these questions is that the "research" step will involve researching information in the passage. Practice with the following passage.

This page left intentionally blank.

Practice Passage

Kidney stones are insoluble aggregate crystals that can form in the urine of certain people. One of the compounds that can contribute to the formation of kidney stones is calcium oxalate (CaC_2O_4, MW = 128.09 g/mol, K_{sp} = 2.3 × 10^{-9}). Oxalic acid is a naturally occurring diprotic acid, ($H_2C_2O_4$, pK_{a1} = 1.3 and pK_{a2} = 4.3) present in foods such as rhubarb and spinach. Oxalic acid can be produced from oxaloacetate, which plays an important role in the citric acid cycle. Uric acid also contributes to the formation of kidney stones, and its crystallization in the joints produces the painful symptoms associated with gout. Uric acid is the final oxidation product of purine metabolism ($H_2C_5H_2N_4O_3$, pK_{a1} = 5.4; pK_{a2} = 10.3). Unlike oxalic acid, uric acid is not completely ionized in normal urine.

If urine becomes supersaturated, seed crystals can aggregate, forming a large mass (stone) in the bladder, the ureters, or the kidneys. Small stones (< 3 mm) are readily passed, however, large stones can cause obstruction and renal colic. In many cases ultrasound can be used to break up stones, but for very large, dense stones, surgery may be required.

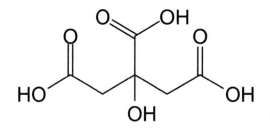

Figure 1. Citric acid ($H_3C_6H_5O_7$)

Reaction 1 Ca^{2+} (aq) + $C_6H_5O_7^{3-}$ (aq) → $CaC_6H_5O_7^{1-}$ (aq)

Urine contains a number of natural chelating agents, such as citrate. These agents are polydentate ligands (Lewis bases) that coordinate to a metal ion and form soluble coordination compounds that help prevent the nucleation and precipitation of calcium oxalate. Figure 1 shows citric acid, a weak acid (pK_{a1} = 3.1, pK_{a2} = 4.8 and pK_{a3} = 6.4). The equilibrium constant at physiological temperature for the formation of the calcium citrate complex ion (Reaction 1) is 1.9 × 10^3. The calcium citrate complex has a residual negative charge that enhances its solubility in aqueous solution.

1. Which of the following formulas best represents the predominant form that exists in solution when citric acid is dissolved in normal urine whose pH is approximately 7.
   A. $H_3C_6H_5O_7$
   B. $H_2C_6H_5O_7^{1-}$
   C. $HC_6H_5O_7^{2-}$
   D. $C_6H_5O_7^{3-}$

2. According to the passage, which temperature range corresponds to the physiological formation of the calcium citrate complex?
   A. 30-32°F
   B. 73-75°F
   C. 98-100°F
   D. 210-212°F

3. Based on information in the passage, what is the equilibrium constant for the following reaction?

$$CaC_2O_4 \text{ (s)} + C_6H_5O_7^{3-} \text{ (aq)} \rightarrow CaC_6H_5O_7^{1-} \text{ (aq)} + C_2O_4^{2-} \text{ (aq)}$$

    A. 4.3×10^8
    B. 1.9×10^3
    C. 4.4×10^{-6}
    D. 2.3×10^{-9}

4. If equimolar solutions of oxalic acid, uric acid, citric acid and urea are prepared, which solution will have the lowest pH?
    A. Oxalic acid, because its first acid dissociation constant is the largest.
    B. Uric acid, because its pK_{a2} value is the largest.
    C. Citric acid, because it is a triprotic acid.
    D. Urea, because it is a basic compound.

5. DNA is made of nucleotides, which utilize non-covalent interactions, such as hydrogen bonding, to form base-pairs. Which of the following nucleotides could produce uric acid as a result of metabolism?
    I. Adenine
    II. Guanine
    III. Glucose
    A. I only
    B. II only
    C. I and II only
    D. I, II and III

Practice Passage Explanations

Kidney stones are insoluble aggregate crystals that can form in the urine of certain people. One of the compounds that can contribute to the formation of kidney stones is calcium oxalate (CaC_2O_4, MW = 128.09 g/mol, $K_{sp} = 2.3 \times 10^{-9}$). Oxalic acid is a naturally occurring diprotic acid, ($H_2C_2O_4$, $pK_{a1} = 1.3$ and $pK_{a2} = 4.3$) present in foods such as rhubarb and spinach. Oxalic acid can be produced from oxaloacetate, which plays an important role in the citric acid cycle. Uric acid also contributes to the formation of kidney stones, and its crystallization in the joints produces the painful symptoms associated with gout. Uric acid is the final oxidation product of purine metabolism ($H_2C_5H_2N_4O_3$, $pK_{a1} = 5.4$; $pK_{a2} = 10.3$). Unlike oxalic acid, uric acid is not completely ionized in normal urine.

Key terms: kidney stone, aggregate, oxaloacetate

Cause and effect: purine metabolism → uric acid → kidney stones

Contrast: oxalic acid ionized in urine, uric is not

If urine becomes supersaturated, seed crystals can aggregate, forming a large mass (stone) in the bladder, the ureters, or the kidneys. Small stones (< 3 mm) are readily passed, however, large stones can cause obstruction and renal colic. In many cases ultrasound can be used to break up stones, but for very large, dense stones, surgery may be required.

Key terms: Supersaturated, bladder, ureters, kidneys, renal colic, and ultrasound

Cause and effect: supersaturated solution → stone formation; small = passed; large = blockage, must be broken up U/S or surgery

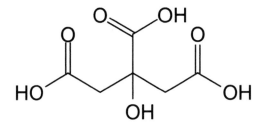

Figure 1. Citric acid ($H_3C_6H_5O_7$)

Figure 1 shows three carboxylic acid groups, which would be ionizable

Reaction 1 $\qquad Ca^{2+}$ (aq) $+ C_6H_5O_7^{3-}$ (aq) $\rightarrow CaC_6H_5O_7^{1-}$ (aq)

Reaction 1 shows the formation of citrate, which ↓ free Ca^{2+} in solution and reduces the possibility of precipitation

Urine contains a number of natural chelating agents, such as citrate. These agents are polydentate ligands (Lewis bases) that coordinate to a metal ion and form soluble coordination compounds that help prevent the nucleation and precipitation of calcium oxalate. Figure 1 shows citric acid, a weak acid ($pK_{a1} = 3.1$, $pK_{a2} = 4.8$ and $pK_{a3} = 6.4$). The equilibrium constant at physiological temperature for the formation of the calcium citrate complex ion (Reaction 1) is 1.9×10^3. The calcium citrate complex has a residual negative charge that enhances its solubility in aqueous solution.

Key terms: chelating agents, polydentate ligands, nucleation

Cause and effect: chelating ligands (Lewis bases) → complex w/ metal → prevent kidney stone (by removing free Ca^{2+} from solution

1) D is correct. **Read:** Which of the following formulas best represents the predominant form that exists in solution when citric acid is dissolved in normal urine whose pH is approximately 7.

Rephrase: With a pH 7, what form does citric acid take?

Research: The passage tells me the three pK_a values for citric acid are $pK_{a1} = 3.1$, $pK_{a2} = 4.8$ and $pK_{a3} = 6.4$. Our outside knowledge tells us that when the pH is higher than the pK_a, the solution is basic relative to the molecule. Outside knowledge also tells us that a basic environment will deprotonate the molecule.

Respond: We can predict the answer without even looking at the choices—a full deprotonated form of citric acid. Citric acid has three acidic protons, and if we remove all of them, the molecule will have a -3 charge. The only one that fits the bill is choice D.

2) C is correct. **Read:** According to the passage, which temperature range corresponds to the physiological formation of the calcium citrate complex?

Rephrase: What temperature is "physiological"?

Research: We don't even need to look back at the passage, since our outside knowledge tells us that the temperature for physiological reactions is 37°C or around 98°F.

Respond: Only choice C fits our outside knowledge.

3) C is correct. **Read:** Based on information in the passage, what is the equilibrium constant for the following reaction?

$$CaC_2O_4 \text{ (s)} + C_6H_5O_7^{3-} \text{ (aq)} \rightarrow CaC_6H_5O_7^{1-} \text{ (aq)} + C_2O_4^{2-} \text{ (aq)}$$

Rephrase: I need to figure out the K_{eq} for an equation not given in the passage.

Research: The reaction given in the question is the sum of solubility reaction for calcium oxalate and the formation reaction for calcium citrate. The corresponding equilibrium constants for these reactions are given in the passage:

$$CaC_2O_4 \text{ (s)} \rightarrow Ca^{2+} \text{ (aq)} + C_2O_4^{2-} \text{ (aq)} \qquad\qquad K_{sp} = 2.3 \times 10^{-9}$$

$$Ca^{2+} \text{ (aq)} + C_6H_5O_7^{3-} \text{ (aq)} \rightarrow CaC_6H_5O_7^{1-} \text{ (aq)} \qquad\qquad K_f = 1.9 \times 10^3$$

$$CaC_2O_4 \text{ (s)} + C_6H_5O_7^{3-} \text{ (aq)} + Ca^{2+} \text{ (aq)} \rightarrow CaC_6H_5O_7^{1-} \text{ (aq)} + Ca^{2+} \text{ (aq)} + C_2O_4^{2-} \text{ (aq)} \qquad K_{eq} = K_{sp} \times K_f$$

From our outside knowledge, we know that we can cancel the calcium ion that appears on both sides of the reaction, which then gives the reaction required in the question. Therefore, multiplying the two equilibrium constants, K_{sp} and K_f will give the equilibrium constant for the desired reaction.

$$K_{sp} \times K_f = (2.3 \times 10^{-9})(1.9 \times 10^3) \approx 2 \times 10^{-9} (2 \times 10^3) = 4 \times 10^{-6}$$

Respond: We have predicted the answer and can thus go right to choice C.

4) A is correct. **Read:** If equimolar solutions of oxalic acid, uric acid, citric acid and urea are prepared, which solution will have the lowest pH?

Rephrase: Low pH means lots of dissociated protons. Equimolar means we don't need to worry about having different concentrations of the molecules in question.

Research: From outside knowledge, we know that to get more dissociated protons, we want a stronger acid, and strong acids have low pK_a's. We then research the passage to find out the needed information. Oxalic acid, uric acid and citric acid are all weak acids, the acidity of which can be measured by the first ionization constant or pK_{a1}. Of the choices and information presented in the passage, oxalic acid is the most acidic since it has the smallest pK_{a1} (thus the largest K_{a1}) and would produce the lowest pH.

Respond: Once again, we know which acid is the strongest and can go right to choice A.

5) **Read:** DNA is made of nucleotides, which utilize non-covalent interactions, such as hydrogen bonding, to form base-pairs. Which of the following nucleotides could produce uric acid as a result of metabolism?

Rephrase: Which nucleotides get metabolized into uric acid?

Research: We may not know this from outside knowledge, but fortunately the passage tells us that purine metabolism can produce uric acid. From there, we just look to our outside knowledge—which nucleotides are purines, and we're done!

Respond: Both A and G are purines, so we can select choice C right away.

3. Must Knows

> Take a systematic approach to answering science questions.
> - Start by reading *exactly* what the question asks.
> - Then *rephrase* the question in your own terms, cutting out extraneous information.
> - Do the necessary *research* relying either on the passage or outside knowledge.
> - Finally, *respond* to the question using either prediction or elimination.

Experimental Design

CHAPTER 7

0. Introduction

Constructing an experiment isn't just a matter of getting the Mythbusters crew together and playing with some toys in the workshop. Good scientific research involves very careful application of the scientific method and research procedures. At the beginning of the book we started by introducing a basic framework for the scientific method, but we will expand on it here.

The process is carried out as follows:

1. Generate a question about the world based on some confusing phenomenon, previous scientific work, or speculation.

Often science research starts because something's confusing—we don't understand why something works out the way it does. An anomaly in research data, an area not covered by our current theories, etc.

For example, a social science researcher might wonder, "Why do girls perform worse on standardized tests of math, even though they often get better grades and more schooling?"

2. Do background research

You don't just jump right from a question to a test. You first have to investigate the issue to see what others have already discovered.

In our example, the researcher might uncover the notion of Stereotype Threat when it comes to performance on standardized tests. She might see that certain minority groups will perform worse on a test due to anxiety about conforming to a negative stereotype, and decide to investigate whether that also happens to girls on math tests.

3. Construct a hypothesis in the form of an if/then statement.

The hypothesis is the researcher's prediction about what the answer to the question is. In our example it might be, "If girls experience stereotype threat with respect to math performance, then they will perform worse on a math test than they otherwise would."

4. Construct and conduct experiments to test the hypothesis and interpret the data.

This is the step that most people think of when they imagine scientists at work—the process of carrying out research protocols and doing statistical analysis of the data. While this certainly can make up the bulk of the time, money, and effort, we mustn't forget about all of the work that came before. Often scientists will say that what makes a great scientist is someone how knows how to "ask the right questions", rather than simply carry out good protocols. In our example, the scientists might give a series of math tests to subjects with differing instructions at the beginning to see if stereotype threat has an effect.

5. Publish and verify the results.

To enter the realm of "scientific knowledge" the information needs to be disseminated, typically in a peer-reviewed journal. Others who work in the field can then review the work and carry things forward, by designing their own research around whatever new questions are raised by the study.

1. Constructing Science Research

When designing one's experiments, there are several factors to consider when developing the research question. One set of criteria that has been suggested is the PICOT criteria:

Population: what specific patient population will be investigated?

Intervention: what is the intervention that will be carried out on these patients?

Comparison group: who will your intervention group be compared against?

Outcome: what is the outcome that will be measured?

Time: what is the appropriate timeline to follow up with subjects?

In addition to these criteria for evaluating your research question, the practicality and value of the research itself can be evaluated with the FINER criteria:

Feasible: is the research in question feasible given time and budget constraints?

Interesting: would the results be interesting to the researcher and the scientific community?

Novel: is this research investigating something new?

Ethical: would this procedure be acceptable to the institutional review board and does it meet the ethical standard of the professional community and the community at large?

Relevant: is this work relevant to current state of scientific knowledge and to future research?

Controls

When constructing an experiment, it is essential to have a control group. We've all been told that over and over in our science classes, but it's important to remember why. The simple act of carrying out an experiment may itself change the results—such that we end up seeing results that are not due to whatever new thing we're testing, but simply occur by virtue of doing the study itself. We should also remember that the materials we use in the lab are not flawless. A control is one way to make sure we didn't get a "bad batch" of something that we ordered from the supply company.

Let's consider a hypothetical study on the doubling time of cells in culture. A scientist begins by growing the cells in a standard nutrient broth and finding that it takes them 21.2 minutes to double. He checks this against the previous literature and sees that the typical doubling time for these types of cells is anywhere from 18 to 22 minutes. So this control shows him that his cells are a normal batch and there's nothing wrong with his nutrient broth, his test tubes, etc. This is an example of a **negative control**. These cells were not altered in any way, and the dependent variable—doubling time—was unchanged, as expected.

Next, he wishes to test the effect of drug X, a new drug that should hypothetically interfere with a certain metabolic pathway. It is well known that drug Q, another drug on the market, does interfere with that pathway. So in his second test, the scientist administers drug Q and notices that the doubling time increased to 36 minutes. This is a **positive control**—something was done in the experiment where it is known that the dependent variable will change. Here, the scientist has established that his cells respond in the expected way to having the metabolic pathway disrupted by drug Q.

Finally, he can test drug X. If he administers it and sees the doubling time increase above 21.2 minutes, he knows that the drug has had an effect. If the results are similar to those for drug Q, the hypothesis that it interferes with the same pathway is slightly strengthened.

In medical studies with human patients, the typical positive control is the current standard of care. The typical negative control would be a placebo pill.

Causation

It's usually almost impossible to prove causation in studies—especially social science studies—with human subjects. There are simply too many variables to control all of them. With social science research, we seek to establish a strong correlation—a relationship between the independent and dependent variables.

In basic science research, where the experimenters can tightly control all relevant variables, it is often much easier to establish causality. To do so, experimenters demonstrate that a change in the independent variable leads to a change in the dependent variable. By showing that the change in the independent variable always leads to the same result in the dependent variable—and then also showing that the result doesn't occur in the absence of the change to the independent variable—basic science researchers can establish causality.

Error, Precision, and Accuracy

Error can creep into an experiment from a number of sources. First, the experimenters or subjects may allow their biases, either consciously or unconsciously, to affect the results. This is discussed more below with double-blind trials. Next, an experimenter may overtly express bias by choosing to either ignore data that don't fit the hypothesis, or choosing not to publish results that don't fit the researcher's own biases.

An example of this is detection bias, in which a researcher is more likely to detect something that fits with his or her previous notions. For example, a physician may be aware that there is a higher incidence of HIV infection in a certain sub-group of his patients. When he sees a new patient who is a member of that sub-group, he may be more likely to screen for HIV, thus skewing the epidemiological data.

The **Hawthorne effect**, or **observation bias**, creeps in when the subjects alter their behavior simply because they know they're being observed. For example, in a study of new diet plans, people participating in the study may alter other lifestyle habits—exercise, sleep patterns, etc.—simply because they know they're being assessed for the effectiveness of a diet.

Next, error can be the systematic result of instruments that give faulty readings or measurements that are being made incorrectly. The goal in collecting data should be to be both accurate and precise.

Accuracy or validity is how close the data collected is to the true value. If a given instrument or measure is able to generate a series of results that are clustered around the true value, then the results are said to be accurate.

Precision or reliability refers to the ability of a measure to give consistent results in a narrow range of possible results. If the measure or instrument gives the same results under the same conditions every time, it is a very precise measure.

It is possible for results to be accurate, but not precise, and vice versa:

Accurate, precise: the results are close to the true value and tightly clumped around the true value.

Accurate, imprecise: the results are close to the true value but are clumped very loosely (would have a large standard deviation).

Inaccurate, precise: the measurements are very tightly clustered, but not around the true value (usually the result of a mis-calibrated instrument).

Inaccurate, imprecise: the results are clumped very loosely around the wrong answer.

2. Research Ethics and Human Subjects

In the Psychological Foundations sections, you're likely to encounter experiments involving human subjects. There are very strict rules about the ethics of experiments involving human subjects. The core ethical concept to be aware of is **informed consent**, in which the subject is adequately informed about the nature of the process, and then is mentally and legally competent to give consent to it.

This core concept of informed consent falls under the general umbrella of respect for autonomy. Broadly speaking, there are four ethical categories that medical intervention (whether experimental or not) must meet: beneficence, acting for the good of the person receiving treatment; nonmaleficence, doing no harm (or least not doing more harm than good); social justice, treating similar patients similarly and working to ensure equal distribution of healthcare resources; and finally respect for autonomy, allowing patients to make decisions based on informed consent.

These broad ethical categories also include other general requirements in medical intervention:

> Honesty
> Confidentiality
> Special protection for vulnerable populations (children, prisoners, the disabled)

> Differences in care may not be based on factors such as race, religion, gender, or sexual orientation
> Assessments must be carried out in the least invasive and potentially harmful manner

Human Subjects

When carrying out the classic experimental approach, researchers will vary the independent variable and measure the dependent variable, as they would in any experiment. Alternatively, researchers can conduct observational experiments.

Because people are not petri dishes, it would be impossible (and unethical) to attempt to control them with the level of precision used in a test tube. As such, the data more often leads to correlations rather than causal conclusions.

Researchers gather data and then use regression analysis to determine the relationships between the variables. Researchers will investigate data that is binary (yes vs. no), continuous (performance on an IQ test), or categorical (race, gender). Regression analysis is discussed further below.

More commonly in the social sciences, researchers carry out observational studies. This is often because carrying out an experimental study would be impossible or unethical (e.g. it would be impossible to change someone's race or religion, and it would unethical to even try). Observational studies vary on how they observe the subjects: forward in time, backward in time, or at one point in time.

Studies that look forward in time are cohort studies. They divide groups into cohorts based on some factor (male vs. female, high educational attainment vs. low) and follow the cohorts over many years, checking in with them periodically to assess outcomes. Studies that look backwards in time are case-control studies. Here, people are identified who have already developed the outcome of interest and then researchers look back to see if a person had a given risk factor. Those "cases" are then compared against "controls" who don't have the disease. For example, researchers might examine 50 children who were born with low birth weight and 50 who weren't, and then look back at the prenatal care the mother received.

Finally, studies that examine people at a given point in time are cross-sectional studies. Those simply gather data on a large cross-section of a group at a particular time, and ask a question at that point in time. For example, a cross-sectional study might look at 5 year olds who are in pre-school programs and those who aren't, and compare their developmental progress at that point.

Because observational studies only lend themselves to correlations, the data must be very strong to suggest that there is an underlying causal connection. The relationship must be linked in time (with the cause always preceding the effect). It must be a strong, consistent, and proportional relationship (meaning if there's more of the cause, there's more of the effect). The connection must be consistent with past research, plausible, and alternatives must have been ruled out. If all of these criteria have been met, researchers may be able to deduce a causal relationship from correlation data.

Should we Treat?

When research has been completed and the data compiled, it then leads to the question as to whether the studied intervention should actually be carried out in patients. First, the data must have the statistical power to indicate that the studied intervention actually had an effect. But more importantly, researchers will need to determine whether the treatment is clinically relevant. After all, a new surgical procedure may have a statistically significant change—say a 3.5 day average recovery time instead of a 3.75 day average recovery time—but such a change may be irrelevant to overall patient health.

When considering whether or not a new treatment modality should be implemented, clinicians must consider factors such as:

> - Cost—if a new treatment costs ten times more, but is only marginally more effective, then it may be unethical to use a treatment that will put the patient in great financial distress for only marginal gains.
> - Side effects—a treatment may be more effective but have side effects that are so deleterious that they create a net decrease in patient well-being.
> - Accessibility—if a patient would, for example, be required to fly across the country to access the treatment, removing them from the social supports of family and friends, it may not be the best choice.
> - Pain, inconvenience, intrusiveness—the overall process of receiving the treatment should not create a "treatment that is worse than the disease" situation for the patient; even an improvement in outcomes may not be worth it for the patient if the treatment is lengthy, painful, and intrusive.

PACS

3. Practical Concerns: The Math and the Money

Finally, we should consider some practical concerns about experimental design. Researchers don't have an infinite amount of time, money, or manpower. They must also be wary of unintended biases and be sure that what they're studying is actually proving what they're setting out to prove.

Statistical Measures in Experiments

In addition to the basic numerical statistics discussed in an earlier chapter, the MCAT will expect you to be familiar with the various statistical tests used by researchers to demonstrate that their findings are real. You won't have to actually calculate the various factors discussed below, but you'll need to be familiar with them. These are all part of the practical considerations in the construction and evaluation of experiments. After all, an experiment whose results cannot be analyzed statistically is often near-useless to researchers.

Independent, Dependent, and Confounding Variables

Variables are the things measured by researchers in the course of their experiments. Independent variables are the ones the researchers directly manipulate, and dependent variables are the ones they measure. Typically, such data is represented graphically with the independent variable graphed along the x-axis and the dependent variable graphed along the y-axis.

Independent variables might include time, temperature, age, socioeconomic status, or organism size. Dependent variables are whatever effect the researchers are looking for. In the social sciences that might be something like IQ, income, symptoms, etc.

A confounding variable is one that the researchers did not account for in their experiment and which alters their results. An example might be a study that analyzes the effects of stereotype bias on math performance by race, but that fails to account for socioeconomic class. Any results obtained would be suspect, since participants may have scored more poorly simply because they were from a lower socioeconomic class, not due to their race.

In the hard sciences, an experiment designed to test two chemistry mechanisms might have a confounding variable of pH if one of the chemicals produces a side product that is an acid and the researchers failed to properly buffer their solutions to prevent changes in pH. In the social sciences, an experiment that showed a correlation between household income and children's college completion could not make the causal assertion that "having higher income causes you to be more likely to complete college." A confounding factor might be that having parents who went to college makes it more likely that the children will complete college. Or having parents with a certain personality style both makes them more likely to have a higher income *and* have children who complete college.

Sampling and Bias

Sample size (usually denoted with N) is simply the number of data points developed in an experiment. In the social sciences and biology, this usually means the number of people or number of organisms in the experiment. The larger the sample size, the higher the statistical power of the experiment. While more is always better, it is usually impossible to test every possible case or every possible person, so a smaller sample of the whole must be taken.

The group of every possible person or organism is the population, out of which the sample is selected. The population could be very broad—every single human would have many billions in the population—or it could be much narrower. The population of 25 year old females living in France with North African ancestry who have completed college and self-identify as queer would be a much smaller population.

Typically, experimenters try to take a random sample of the population under study, simply because studying every single individual would be impossible. If researchers wished to assess the levels of DDT present in hawks, they could not capture and assess every hawk. Instead, they would have to capture a random group of hawks and test them, and then extrapolate to the whole population.

When researchers attempt to generate a random sample but instead get a biased, or non-random sample, an error can be introduced into the results. One example of such an unintended biased sample was in the polling results for the 2008 US presidential elections. Polling companies called people before the election to ask them who they intended to vote for. But such companies were depending on traditional land lines rather than cell phones. As it turned out, those voters who only used cell phones tended to skew both younger and more Democratic in their voting patterns. As a result, the election resulted in a much bigger win for the Democratic candidate than had been predicted.

Some other common types of bias include: geographic bias (surveying people in only one area), self-selection bias (only surveying those who choose to participate), pre-screening bias (only including those participants who saw the initial screening questions), and healthy population bias (using only people who are more likely than average to be healthy in the study).

The t-test

The t-test is a very common statistical measure used when analyzing experimental data. It's a way to see if the means of two data sets are actually different, or if the difference is simply due to chance. For example, researchers might measure the mean doubling time of a certain bacterial population as 25.2 minutes, then administer a drug and find the new mean doubling time to be 21.5 minutes. Are these two numbers actually different or is the difference merely due to chance?

This is where a t-test would be used. For the MCAT, you won't have to actually know how to calculate a t-test. Instead, you will have to be familiar with the importance of p-values. After performing a t-test and comparing it to a table of p-values, experimenters can determine if the difference they've observed is significant or not. Typically, a p-value must be below 0.05 for any observed difference to be statistically significant. This means that there is only a 5% chance that the observation was due to chance alone, and there is a 95% chance that the observed difference is real.

In our previous example, let's imagine the experimenters found that the p-value for the two means (25.2 minutes and then 21.5 minutes) was 0.15. This would mean that there is an 85% chance that those two numbers really are different, and a 15% chance that the difference observed is just due to random chance. You might think that's pretty good—"Hey, 85% chance of a real difference sounds good to me!" but researchers are a careful, conservative bunch. They only assert that their observations are statistically significant if they're *at least* 95% sure that it's real.

The Null Hypothesis

The tests discussed above are all done in relation to the null hypothesis. The null hypothesis says that whatever we're testing is irrelevant, or not true, or there is no difference between the groups under study. We more often think not of proving our hypothesis, but rather of rejecting the null hypothesis.

For example, let's say we're testing a hypothesis that says that increasing the temperature of a cell broth will lower the doubling time of that population of cells. The null hypothesis would be, "Raising the temperature of a cell broth will have no effect on doubling time." We then set out disprove the null hypothesis. If we can conclusively disprove it, then our original hypothesis is much more likely to be true.

When comparing our results to the null hypothesis, it is possible to get it right or make an error:

1. Type I error = the null hypothesis is true, but we reject it

This is a **false positive**. We think our hypothesis is true, but in reality the null hypothesis is true.

In health care, a false positive can be relatively harmless, or *very* dangerous. For example, you might think you have a fever because you feel flushed, and so you take an aspirin. If you're otherwise healthy, a single aspirin poses no real risk. If it turns out you didn't actually have a fever, then your self-assessment was a false positive, albeit a harmless one. By contrast, a false positive that said a patient has cancer (when in fact she doesn't) could be *very* harmful if it lead to a lengthy and unnecessary round of damaging chemotherapy.

2. Type II error = the null hypothesis is false, but we accept it

This is called a **false negative**. Our hypothesis was true, but we reject it and accept the null hypothesis.

In health care, this would be "missing the diagnosis"—the patient *had* the condition, but we told him that he didn't. Just as with a false positive, a false negative can have consequences that are very mild (if the condition is benign or would clear up on its own) or are fatal.

3. Null hypothesis is true, and we accept the null hypothesis.

This would be an example of confidence. We had a hypothesis, but it was wrong, and we demonstrated that it was wrong. If our results have statistical significance, and the stronger our results are, the more **confidence** our study has.

4. The null hypothesis is false, and we reject the null hypothesis.

Here our hypothesis was true and we figured out that it was true (and that the null hypothesis was wrong). If we have good results and a strong, well-constructed study, we would say our results have power. The better our results, and the more likely that we're right, the more **power** our study has.

Positive and Negative Correlation

When comparing independent and dependent variables, researchers look to see how closely correlated they are. This relationship is expressed as a correlation coefficient (usually denoted R) that ranges from -1 to +1. A correlation value of -1 would indicate perfect negative correlation. A value of +1 indicates perfect positive correlation, and 0 indicates no correlation at all.

A data set with no correlation, when graphed, will not demonstrate any particular relationship:

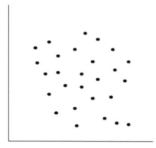

Figure 1. No correlation

Compare that to a data set with a negative correlation. In the figure below, the correlation is a very strong relationship, because the data points all lie very close to the line:

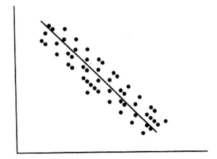

Figure 2. Negative correlation

And finally, here's an example of a positive correlation (in the graph below, R is approximately +0.6):

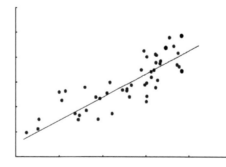

Figure 3. Positive correlation

We remember, though, that correlation does not prove causation. Two things may be correlated—even *perfectly* correlated, even though one does not directly cause the other.

Validity and Reliability

For an experiment or test to have value, it must be both valid and reliable.

Validity is a measure of how well a given experiment is actually measuring what it sets out to measure. If a study has internal validity, then the study has internally been well constructed, using things like large random samples, safeguards against confounding variables, reasonable and reliable processes and instruments, etc. If a study is internally valid, we can then assess whether it has external validity—can the results of the experiment be generalized to other settings. After all, if a study only shows that X is related to Y *for this experimental group*, then it's not very valuable for drawing conclusions about the larger population. To have external validity, an experiment must tightly control any situational variables in the execution of the study. Finally, construct validity refers to how well a given assessment (a survey, a test, etc.) actually measures what it claims to measure—has it been properly constructed to measure the relevant thing.

Reliability refers to how consistent and repeatable an experiment or assessment is. Test-test reliability refers to the fact that a good test should give stable results over time. For example, if you took the MCAT once a year every year without doing any prep or practice (although why on Earth would you want to do something like that?!), you would get basically the same results every time because the MCAT has good test-test reliability. One other form of reliability is inter-rater reliability. That means that if an assessment is carried out by different researchers, they should generate similar results. For example, the SAT includes an essay that a person grades on a scale of 1-6. The SAT essay has good inter-rater reliability because the same essay will be given the same (or nearly the same) score regardless of which person scores it.

Biases and the Double-Blind Randomized Controlled Trial

When conducting research, especially with human subjects, it is extraordinarily easy to skew the results due to unintended biases on the part of the researchers or the subjects. If the subjects know that they're getting a new experimental drug, they may over-state the results due to the placebo effect. If the researchers know which subjects are getting the new treatment and which are getting the placebo, they may unconsciously skew the results through their tone or body language when communicating with patients.

To avoid these problems, researchers use randomized controlled trials, and whenever possible they use a double-blind protocol. In a randomized controlled trial, the subjects are randomly assigned to the experimental group and to the control group. This prevents any bias in who gets assigned to which group. The control group will receive either no treatment, a placebo, or the current standard treatment.

In a blind trial, the patients do not know whether they are receiving the placebo or the experimental treatment. This helps prevent any biased reactions from the subjects. Some people, for example, may feel (perhaps unconsciously) that if they are getting a fancy new experimental treatment, they "should" get better, and so will report a larger improvement in their symptoms than they otherwise would. While a blind trial is helpful, it can still introduce biases through unintended communication from the researchers.

To prevent this, researchers use a double-blind trial in which neither the subjects, nor the researchers, know who is receiving the treatment and who is receiving the control. All of the data identifying which is the control and which is the experimental group are held by a person who is not directly interacting with the patients, and it is only after the data have been collected and analyzed that researchers "remove the blinds" to see what the results show.

5. Must Knows

> Experiments are generated following a set series of steps.
>   – Criteria such as the PICOT or FINER criteria are used.
> Controls can be positive or negative.
> Observation bias, or the Hawthorne effect, is when subjects alter their behavior because they know they are being observed.
> Experiments are run against the null hypothesis—the assumption that there is no difference between the groups being tested.
> Type I error, or false positive, is when our hypothesis was wrong, but we accept it.
> Type II error, or false negative, is when our hypothesis was right, but we reject it.
> Validity relates to how well an experiment is actually testing what it sets out to test, whereas reliability is the consistency or repeatability of an experiment.

This page left intentionally blank.

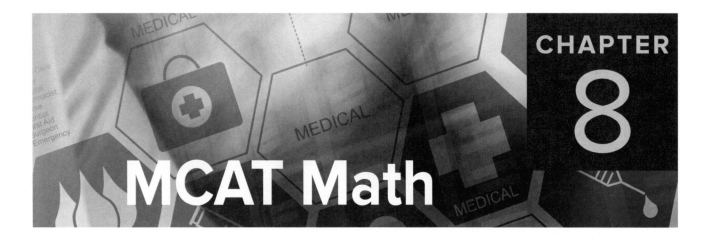

MCAT Math

0. Introduction

Many of us have been using a calculator so long that we've forgotten the fundamentals. Unfortunately, the MCAT is not going to cut us any slack here. The test will expect us to be able to do calculations involving basic functions and approximations with nothing more advanced than a pencil and paper.

The first step is, as ever, assessment. The following section begins with two 100-question assessment quizzes. Take these quizzes and assess your performance. Then continue with the rest of the chapter and the practice questions based on your assessment performance. If you score 90-95%+ correct on both assessments, you can likely skip this entire chapter.

1. Assessments

Arithmetic Assessment

Section 1: Basic operations

1. $13 + 9 =$
2. $27 + 9.6 =$
3. $103 + 19 =$
4. $1152 + 879 =$
5. $989 + 11271 =$
6. $35 - 8 =$
7. $81 - 98 =$
8. $10.7 - 99 =$
9. $23 - 561 =$
10. $415 - 296 =$
11. $8 \times 7 =$
12. $12 \times 3 =$
13. $11 \times 1.1 =$
14. $3 \times 104 =$
15. $20 \times 213 =$
16. $64 / 4 =$
17. $36 / 1.2 =$
18. $3 \times 2 + 1 =$
19. $(4 + 2)(9 \times 1.8) =$
20. $4 / 2 + 1 \times 9 - 5 =$

Section 2: Fractions

1. $25 / 5 =$
2. $1/3 + 4/3 =$
3. $1/3 + 2/5 =$
4. $4/7 + 1/4 =$
5. $16/19 - 1/2 =$
6. $2/3 - 3/5 =$
7. $1/4 - 5/6 =$
8. $1/2 \times 1/3 =$
9. $4/9 \times 0.1 =$
10. $13/2 \times 2/13 =$
11. $1/2 \div 1/3 =$
12. $2/3 \div 3/2 =$
13. $12/5 \div 1/2 =$
14. $7/8 \div 5/4 =$
15. $3/4 \times 0.15 =$
16. $1/3 \div 1/5 \times 5/4 =$
17. $2/3 + 2/9 \times 1/3 =$
18. $1/4 \div 1/3 + 0.5 =$
19. $(4/5 + 0.2) \times 8/9 =$
20. $1/2 + 1/2 =$

Section 3: Percentages

1. 50% of $30 =$
2. 25% of $48 =$
3. 75% of $3/4 =$
4. 80% of 15% of $1,000 =$
5. 45% of $(9/10 \times 0.2) =$
6. 50% more than $50 =$
7. 10% more than $25 =$
8. 25% sale off an item that starts at $40 =$
9. A student scores 87% on a test of 200 questions. He got wrong =
10. A car starts at 50 mph, increases its speed by 10% and then decreases its speed by 10%. It ends at =
11. 15% less than $90 =$
12. 30% less than $0.0045 =$
13. 1.2% of $50 =$
14. 2.5% of $10.1 =$
15. A class of 40 students is 60% boys and among the boys 50% play soccer. The number of non-soccer playing boys is =
16. 10% of the sale price of a house is commission paid to the real estate agent. A house sells for $250,000. The real estate agent receives =
17. 36.6% of $1000 =$
18. 50% more than 10% less than $50 =$
19. 20% less than 25% more than $40 =$
20. 100% of $100 =$

Section 4: Roots, Scientific Notation

1. $4^2 =$
2. $11^2 =$
3. $105.23^0 =$
4. $0^{13} =$
5. $2^2 + 3^3 =$
6. $10^5 / 10^2 =$
7. $(5^2)^2 \times 5^{11} =$
8. $2^3 \times 4^3 =$
9. $1^5 + 2^4 + 3^3 =$
10. $\sqrt{169} =$
11. $\sqrt{4} + \sqrt{16} =$
12. $\sqrt{5} \times \sqrt{5} =$
13. $\sqrt{144} - \sqrt{25} =$
14. $\sqrt{32} =$
15. $\sqrt{50} =$
16. $\sqrt{(4/9)} =$
17. $3.2 \times 10^4 + 3.2 \times 10^4 =$
18. $2 \times 10^2 \times (4 \times 10^6)^2 =$
19. $1.5 \times 10^5 - 9.8 \times 10^4 =$
20. $\sqrt{(2.5 \times 10^9)} =$

Section 5: Estimation

21. $25.113 + 24.98 \approx$
22. $30.013 + 0.995 \approx$
23. $119.155 - 247.03 \approx$
24. $4.814 \times 9.21 \approx$
25. $1.0311 \times 483.3 \approx$
26. $1021.4 / 511.1 \approx$
27. $8.33332 / 29.4 \approx$
28. 31.14% of $99.8 \approx$
29. 91.66% more than $1044 \approx$
30. 12.555% less than $94.3 \approx$
31. $4.1^2 \approx$
32. $5^{2.01} \approx$
33. $2^{3.8} \approx$
34. $\sqrt{98} \approx$
35. $\sqrt{160} \approx$
36. $\sqrt{38} + \sqrt{45} \approx$
37. $4.9(2.012^2 + \sqrt{24}) \approx$
38. $(51/99) + (31.22/63.998) \approx$
39. $6.022 \times 10^{23} + 9.88 \times 10^{22} \approx$
40. $\sqrt{6 \times 10^{19}} + [9.1 \times 10^4]^2 \approx$

Answer Key

Section 1: Basic operations

1. $13 + 9 = 22$
2. $27 + 9.6 = 36.6$
3. $102 + 19 = 121$
4. $1152 + 879 = 2031$
5. $989 + 11271 = 12260$
6. $35 - 8 = 27$
7. $81 - 98 = -17$
8. $10.7 - 99 = -88.3$
9. $23 - 561 = -538$
10. $415 - 296 = 119$
11. $8 \times 7 = 56$
12. $12 \times 3 = 36$
13. $11 \times 1.1 = 12.1$
14. $3 \times 104 = 312$
15. $20 \times 213 = 4260$
16. $64 / 4 = 16$
17. $36 / 1.2 = 30$
18. $3 \times 2 + 1 = 7$
19. $(4 + 2)(9 \times 1.8) = 97.2$
20. $4 / 2 + 1 \times 9 - 5 = 6$

Section 2: Fractions

1. $25 / 5 = 5$
2. $1/3 + 4/3 = 5/3$
3. $1/3 + 2/5 = 5/15 + 6/15 = 11/15$
4. $4/7 + 1/4 = 16/28 + 7/28 = 23/28$
5. $16/19 - 1/2 = 32/38 - 19/38 = 13/38$
6. $2/3 - 3/5 = 10/15 - 9/15 = 1/15$
7. $1/4 - 5/6 = 3/12 - 10/12 = -7/12$
8. $1/2 \times 1/3 = 1 \times 1 / 2 \times 3 = 1/6$
9. $4/9 \times 0.1 = 4/9 \times 1/10 = 4/90$
10. $13/2 \times 2/13 = 13 \times 2 / 2 \times 13 = 26/26 = 1$
11. $1/2 \div 1/3 = 1/2 \times 3/1 = 3/2$
12. $2/3 \div 3/2 = 2/3 \times 2/3 = 4/9$
13. $12/5 \div 1/2 = 12/5 \times 2/1 = 24/5$
14. $7/8 \div 5/4 = 7/8 \times 4/5 = 28/40 = 14/20 = 7/10$
15. $3/4 \times 0.15 = 3/4 \times 15/100 = 45/400 = 9/80$
16. $1/3 \div 1/5 \times 5/4 = 1/3 \times 5/1 \times 5/4 = 25/12$
17. $2/3 + 2/9 \times 1/3 = 2/3 + 2/27 = 20/27$
18. $1/4 \div 1/3 + 0.5 = 1/4 \times 3/1 + 1/2 = 5/4$
19. $(4/5 + 0.2) \times 8/9 = (4/5 + 1/5)(8/9) = 8/9$
20. $1/2 + 1/2 = 2/2 = 1$

Section 3: Percentages

1. 50% of $30 = 15$
2. 25% of $48 = 12$
3. 75% of $3/4 = 9/16$
4. 80% of 15% of $1,000 = 0.8(150) = 120$
5. 45% of $(9/10 \times 0.2) = 0.45(0.18) = 0.081$
6. 50% more than $50 = 1.5(50) = 75$
7. 10% more than $25 = 1.1(25) = 27.5$
8. 25% sale off an item that starts at $40 = 0.75(40) = 30$
9. A student scores 87% on a test of 200 questions. He got wrong $= 0.13(200) = 26$
10. A car starts at 50 mph, increases its speed by 10% and then decreases its speed by 10%. It ends at $= 0.9(1.1(50)) = 0.9(55) = 49.5$
11. 15% less than $90 = 0.85(90) = 76.5$
12. 30% less than $0.0045 = 0.7(0.0045) = 0.00315$
13. 1.2% of $50 = 0.012(50) = 0.6$
14. 2.5% of $10.1 = 0.025(10.1) = 0.2525$
15. A class of 40 students is 60% boys and among the boys 50% play soccer. The number of non-soccer playing boys is $= 0.5(0.6(40)) = 12$
16. 10% of the sale price of a house is commission paid to the real estate agent. A house sells for $250,000. The real estate agent receives $= \$25,000$
17. 36.6% of $1000 = 366$
18. 50% more than 10% less than $50 = 1.5(0.9(50)) = 67.5$
19. 20% less than 25% more than $40 = 0.8(1.25(40)) = 40$
20. 100% of $100 = 100$

Section 4: Roots, Scientific Notation

1. $4^2 = 16$
2. $11^2 = 121$
3. $105.23^0 = 1$
4. $0^{13} = 0$
5. $2^2 + 3^3 = 4 + 27 = 31$
6. $10^5 / 10^2 = 10^{(5-2)} = 10^3 = 1000$
7. $(5^2)^2 \times 5^{11} = 5^{2 \times 2} \times 5^{11} = 5^4 \times 5^{11} = 5^{(4+11)} = 5^{15}$
8. $2^3 \times 4^3 = (2 \times 4)^3 = 8^3 = 512$
9. $1^5 + 2^4 + 3^3 = 1 + 16 + 27 = 44$
10. $\sqrt{169} = 13$
11. $\sqrt{4} + \sqrt{16} = 2 + 4 = 6$
12. $\sqrt{5} \times \sqrt{5} = \sqrt{(5 \times 5)} = \sqrt{25} = 5$
13. $\sqrt{144} - \sqrt{25} = 12 - 5 = 7$
14. $\sqrt{32} = \sqrt{(16 \times 2)} = \sqrt{16} \times \sqrt{2} = 4\sqrt{2}$
15. $\sqrt{50} = \sqrt{(25 \times 2)} = \sqrt{25} \times \sqrt{2} = 5\sqrt{2}$
16. $\sqrt{(4/9)} = \sqrt{4} / \sqrt{9} = 2/3$
17. $3.2 \times 10^4 + 3.2 \times 10^4 = 6.4 \times 10^4$
18. $2 \times 10^2 \times (4 \times 10^6)^2 = 2 \times 10^2 \times 16 \times 10^{12} = 32 \times 10^{14} = 3.2 \times 10^{15}$
19. $1.5 \times 10^5 - 9.8 \times 10^4 = 15 \times 10^4 - 9.8 \times 10^4 = 5.2 \times 10^4$
20. $\sqrt{(2.5 \times 10^9)} = \sqrt{(25 \times 10^8)} = \sqrt{25} \times \sqrt{10^8} = 5 \times 10^4$

Section 5: Estimation

(for these questions, give yourself credit for a right answer if you were within 10-20% of the solution presented here)

1. $25.113 + 24.98 \approx 25 + 25 = 50$
2. $30.013 + 0.995 \approx 30 + 1 = 31$
3. $119.155 - 247.03 \approx 120 - 250 = -130$
4. $4.814 \times 9.21 \approx 5 \times 9 = 45$
5. $1.0311 \times 483.3 \approx 1 \times 484 = 484$
6. $1021.4 / 511.1 \approx 1000 / 500 = 2$
7. $8.33332 / 29.4 \approx 8 / 29$
8. 31.14% of $99.8 \approx 0.3(100) = 30$
9. 91.66% more than $1044 \approx 2(1000) = 2000$
10. 12.555% less than $94.3 \approx 0.88(100) = 88$
11. $4.1^2 \approx 16$
12. $5^{2.01} \approx 25$
13. $2^{3.8} \approx$ between 8 and 16, closer to 16
14. $\sqrt{98} \approx$ a little less than 10
15. $\sqrt{160} \approx$ between 12 and 13, closer to 13
16. $\sqrt{38} + \sqrt{45} \approx 6.1 + 6.9 = 13$
17. $4.9(2.012^2 + \sqrt{24}) \approx 5(4+5) = 45$
18. $(51/99) + (31.22/63.998) \approx (50/100)+(32/64)=1$
19. $6.022 \times 10^{23} + 9.88 \times 10^{22} \approx 6 \times 10^{23} + 1 \times 10^{23} = 7 \times 10^{23}$
20. $\sqrt{(6 \times 10^{19})} + [9.1 \times 10^4]^2 \approx \sqrt{(60 \times 10^{18})} + 81 \times 10^8 = 7.8 \times 10^9 + 8.1 \times 10^9 = 15.9 \times 10^9 = 1.59 \times 10^{10}$

Performance Analysis

90-100. Good job! Your arithmetic skills are solid. You can likely skip the arithmetic section.

75-89. You got a large majority of the questions correct, but still hit enough trouble that you'll want to invest in a thorough review. Work your way through all of the math sections, carefully review all of the questions and then come back and re-do this assessment.

50-74. You hit some real trouble on this assessment. You'll need to work your way through the math chapter very slowly and carefully. Read it over more than once, make study sheets, and complete the questions at least twice.

<50. You're going to need heavy-duty review to get yourself ready for the MCAT, including work beyond this prep book. Consider picking up additional math review books to build up your fundamentals.

Algebra, Stats, and Trig Assessment

Section 1: Probability and statistics

1. A drawer contains 4 black socks and 10 white socks. What are the odds of drawing out a white sock?
2. A drawer contains 4 black socks and 10 white socks. What are the odds of drawing out two white socks in a row?
3. A fair coin is tossed three times. What are the odds of getting three heads in a row?
4. A fair coin is tossed four times. What are the odds of getting at least one tails?
5. What are the odds of rolling two six-sided dice and getting at least one six?

Questions 6-13 use this data set:

$\{1, 2, 3, 3, 3, 4, 6, 7, 7, 7, 11, 45\}$

6. What is the mode(s) of the set?
7. What is the mean of the set?
8. What is the median of the set?
9. What is the range of the set?
10. If the 45 were replaced with a 4, what would happen to the standard deviation of the set?
11. If the 6 were replaced with a 72, what would happen to the standard deviation of the set?
12. What is the interquartile range of the set?
13. Which data point(s) is/are outlier(s)?

Questions 14-19 use this data set:

$\{5, 5.1, 5.2, 5.3, 5.4, 5.5, 5.6\}$

14. What is the mode(s) of the set?
15. What is the mean of the set?
16. What is the median of the set?
17. What is the range of the set?
18. What is the interquartile range of the set?
19. Which data point(s) is/are outlier(s)?
20. For a given couple's genetic makeup, there is a 1/2 chance that any son will be color blind and a 1/4 chance that any daughter will be colorblind. If the couple has two children, what are the odds that they will have a colorblind son and a color blind daughter?

Section 2: Manipulating equations

21. Isolate d: $v_f^2 = v_i^2 + 2ad$
22. Isolate R: $PV = nRT$
23. Solve for x: $2x/3 + 5 = 5x$
24. Solve for x: $4x/5 = 2/3x$
25. Solve for x: $(5/x) + 10 = 14$
26. Solve for x+y: $5x - 10 = 5 - 5y$
27. Solve for x: $5 / x^2 = 1 / 5$
28. Solve for x: $(\sin 30°)/x = 5$
29. Solve for x:
    a. $x + y = 15$
    b. $3y/2 = 21$
30. Solve for x:
    a. $4x = 3y$
    b. $x = 15 - 3y$
31. Solve for x:
    a. $x(x + 2y) = 9 - y$
    b. $(2y/3) + 1 = 15/9$
32. Solve for v_f / v_i
    a. $v_f^2 = v_i^2 + 2ad$
    b. A car starts at 10 m/s and accelerates at 5 m/s^2 for 10m.
33. Find P_i / P_f
    a. $PV = nRT$
    b. A sample of gas has its volume cut in half and its temperature also cut in half.
34. Find V_i / V_f
    a. $PV = nRT$
    b. A sample of gas has its pressure tripled and its temperature doubled.
35. Find T_i / T_f
    a. $PV = nRT$
    b. A sample of gas has its pressure and volume both doubled.
36. Find F_i / F_f
    a. $F = GMm / r^2$
    b. Mass 1 is doubled and the distance between the masses is tripled.
37. Find F_i / F_f
    a. $F = GMm / r^2$
    b. Both masses are doubled and the distance between the masses is halved.
38. Find F_i / F_f
    a. $F = kQq / r^2$
    b. One charge is doubled, the other is halved, and the distance between the charges is doubled.

39. If a sample of gas has the pressure and temperature held constant, but the volume doubles, then what must be true:
    a. (Use PV = nRT)
40. Solve for x: 2 log x = 10

Section 3: Logarithms

Note: if no base is indicated, then it is the common log, $\log_{10}$

41. $\log_5 5 =$
42. $\log 1 =$
43. $\ln e =$
44. $2.3 \times \log_{10} e \approx$
45. $\log (3 \times 10^4) \approx$
46. $\log (X / Y) =$
47. $\log (1 / Q) =$
48. $\log 100 =$
49. $\log 0.001 =$
50. $\log 10 =$
51. $\log (5 \times 10^5) \approx$
52. $-\log (2.5 \times 10^{-15}) \approx$
53. $-\log (10^5) \approx$
54. $-\log (8 \times 10^{-2}) \approx$
55. $\log 1/100 =$
56. $\log X^Y =$
57. $\log 10^6 - \log 100,000 =$
58. $\log 50 + \log 2 =$
59. $\log 4,000 - \log 40 =$
60. $2 \times \log (\sqrt{10}) =$

Section 4: Trig

61. $\sin 0° =$
62. $\cos 30° =$
63. $\tan 45° =$
64. $\sin 60° =$
65. $\cos 90° =$
66. $\tan 180° =$
67. $\sin 30° =$
68. $\cos 45° =$
69. $\tan 60° =$
70. $\sin^{-1} 1/2 =$
71. $\cos^{-1} 1/2 =$
72. $\tan^{-1} 1 =$
73. $\sin^{-1} \sqrt{3} / 2 =$
74. $\cos^{-1} 0 =$
75. $\tan^{-1} \sqrt{3} =$
76. The hypotenuse of a 30-60-90 triangle is 4.2 meters long. The shorter leg is:

77. One leg of a 45-45-90 triangle is 20 meters long. The other leg is:
78. The longer leg of a 30-60-90 triangle is $\sqrt{6}$ meters long. The shorter leg is:
79. The hypotenuse of a 45-45-90 triangle is $6\sqrt{2}$ meters long. The sum of the lengths of the legs is:
80. $(\sin 30°)^2 + (\cos 30°)^2 =$

Section 5: Units

Note: for the following, use the following conversion factors:

    1 yard = 3 feet = 36 inches
    1 inch = 2.5 cm
    1 Calorie = 1000 calories = 4184 J
    1 pound (lb) = 4.45 N

81. 15.2 cm in mm =
82. 1,500 μJ in kJ =
83. 3.2 Gg in kg =
84. 0.0041 Ms in ms =
85. 2 m in inches =
86. 25 cm in inches =
87. A garden is designed to be 2 yards long and 6 yards wide. How many square feet is this:
88. An apartment is advertised as being 1881 square feet. This is how many square yards:
89. A meal is advertised as containing 100 Calories. How many joules is this:
90. To boil a certain cup of water will take 836800 J of energy. How many calories is this:
91. On earth, a person's weight is 100 pounds. On the moon, the person's weight in Newtons would be (approximate the gravitational force on the Moon as 1/5 that of Earth):
92. A bag of building materials weighs 8900 N. How many pounds is this:
93. An experiment is carried out at 298K. This is how many °C?
94. The boiling point of water in F, °C, and K is:
95. A car is able to drive 350 miles on a single tank of gas and the tank holds 15 gallons. How many miles per gallon does the car get:
96. A recipe calls for 10 g of flour and 20 g of sugar. A cook wishes to make 100 portions of this recipe. Flour is sold in 500g bags and sugar is sold in 250 g bags. The minimum number of bags of flour and sugar needed is:

97. 1 mile is 1.6 km and 1 gallon is 3.8 L. A car gets 40 miles per gallon. How many km per liter is this?

98. A butterfly flies at 24 inches per second. How many meters per minute is this?

99. The average adult human needs to consume 2000 Calories per day to maintain weight. How many joules per minute is this?

100. The freezing point of water in F, °C, and K is:

Answer Key

Section 1: Probability and statistics

1. A drawer contains 4 black socks and 10 white socks. What are the odds of drawing out a white sock?

   10 / 14

2. A drawer contains 4 black socks and 10 white socks. What are the odds of drawing out two white socks in a row?

   10/14 x 9/13 = 90 / 182 = 45 / 91

3. A fair coin is tossed three times. What are the odds of getting three heads in a row?

   1/2 x 1/2 x 1/2 = 1/8

4. A fair coin is tossed four times. What are the odds of getting at least one tails?

   No tails at all:
   1/2 x 1/2 x 1/2 x 1/2 = 1/16
   At least one tails = 1 – 1/16 = 15/16.

5. What are the odds of rolling two six-sided dice and getting at least one six?

   1/6 + 1/6 – 1/36 = 11/36

Questions 6-13 use this data set:

{1, 2, 3, 3, 3, 4, 6, 7, 7, 7, 11, 45}

6. What is the mode(s) of the set?

   3 and 7

7. What is the mean of the set?

   8.25

8. What is the median of the set?

   (4+6)/2 = 5

9. What is the range of the set?

   45 – 1 = 44

10. If the 45 were replaced with a 4, what would happen to the standard deviation of the set?

    Decreased standard deviation

11. If the 6 were replaced with a 72, what would happen to the standard deviation of the set?

    An increased standard deviation

12. What is the interquartile range of the set?

    75th percentile = 7
    25th percentile = 3
    IR = 7-3 = 4

13. Which data point(s) is/are outlier(s)?

    The only outlier is the 45

Questions 14-19 use this data set:

{5, 5.1, 5.2, 5.3, 5.4, 5.5, 5.6}

14. What is the mode(s) of the set?

    No mode

15. What is the mean of the set?

    5.3

16. What is the median of the set?

    5.3

17. What is the range of the set?

    5.6 – 5 = 0.6

18. What is the interquartile range of the set?

    IR = 5.5-5.1 = 0.4

19. Which data point(s) is/are outlier(s)?

    No outliers

20. For a given couple's genetic makeup, there is a 1/2 chance that any son will be colorblind and a 1/4 chance that any daughter will be colorblind. If the couple has two children, what are the odds that they will have a colorblind son and a colorblind daughter?

    Two ways for this outcome:
    The first child is a son (1/2) who is colorblind (1/2) and the second child is a daughter (1/2) who is color blind (1/4) = 1/2 x 1/2 x 1/2 x 1/4 = 1/32
    The first child is a daughter (1/2) who is colorblind (1/4) and the second child is a son (1/2) who is color blind (1/2) = 1/2 x 1/4 x 1/2 x 1/2 = 1/32
    1/32 + 1/32 = 1/16

Section 2: Manipulating equations

21. Isolate d: $v_f^2 = v_i^2 + 2ad$

    $d = (v_f^2 – v_i^2)/2a$

22. Isolate R: $PV = nRT$

    $R = PV/nT$

23. Solve for x: 2x/3 + 5 = 5x

    2x + 15 = 15x
    15 = 13x
    x = 15/13

24. Solve for x: 4x/5 = 2/3x

    Cross multiply:
    $12x^2 = 10$
    $x^2 = 10/12 = 5/6$
    $x = \sqrt{(5/6)}$

25. Solve for x: (5/x) + 10 = 14

    5/x = 4
    4x = 5
    x = 5/4

26. Solve for x+y: $5x - 10 = 5 - 5y$

    $5x + 5y - 10 = 5$

    $5x + 5y = 15$

    $x + y = 3$

27. Solve for x: $5 / x^2 = 1 / 5$

    Cross multiply:

    $x^2 = 25$

    $x = 5$

28. Solve for x: $(\sin 30°)/x = 5$

    $(1/2)/x = 5$

    $1/2 = 5x$

    $x = 1/10$

29. Solve for x:

    $x + y = 15$

    $3y/2 = 21$

    $3y = 42$

    $y = 14$

    $x + 14 = 15$

    $x = 1$

30. Solve for x:

    $4x = 3y$

    $x = 15 - 3y$

    $4(15 - 3y) = 3y$

    $60 - 12y = 3y$

    $60 = 15y$

    $y = 4$

    $4x = 3(4)$

    $x = 3$

31. Solve for x:

    $x(x + 2y) = 9 - y$

    $(2y/3) + 1 = 15/9$

    $2y/3 = 15/9 - 1$

    $2y/3 = 15/9 - 9/9$

    $2y/3 = 6/9 = 2/3$

    $2y = 2$

    $y = 1$

    $x(x + 2(1)) = 9 - 1$

    $x(x+2) = 8$

    $x^2 + 2x - 8 = 0$

    $(x+4)(x-2) = 0$

    $x = 2$ or -4

32. Solve for v_f / v_i

    $v_f^2 = v_i^2 + 2ad$

    A car starts at 10 m/s and accelerates at 5 m/s^2 for 10m.

    $v_f^2 = (10)^2 + 2(5)(10) = 100 + 100$

    $v_f = \sqrt{200}$

    $v_f / v_i = \sqrt{200} / 10 = \sqrt{200} / \sqrt{100} = \sqrt{(200/100)} = \sqrt{2} \approx 1.4$

33. Find P_i / P_f

    $PV = nRT$

    A sample of gas has the volume cut in half and the temperature also cut in half.

    $V_f = 0.5V_i$

    $T_f = 0.5T_i$

    $P_i / P_f = (nRT_i / V_i) / (nRT_f / V_f)$

    $= (T_i / V_i) / (0.5T_i / 0.5V_i)$

    $= (T_i / V_i) \times (0.5V_i / 0.5T_i)$

    $= 0.5 / 0.5 = 1$

34. Find V_i / V_f

    $PV = nRT$

    A sample of gas has the pressure tripled and the temperature doubled.

    $P_f = 3P_i$

    $T_f = 2T_i$

    $V_i / V_f = (nRT_i / P_i) / (nRT_f / P_f)$

    $= (T_i / P_i) / (T_f / P_f)$

    $= (T_i / P_i) / (2T_i / 3P_i)$

    $= (T_i / P_i) \times (3P_i / 2T_i)$

    $= 3/2$

35. Find T_i / T_f

    $PV = nRT$

    A sample of gas has the pressure and volume both doubled.

    Doubling both P and V will quadruple the left side of the equation. To maintain the equation the right side must also quadruple. So T_f is four times T_i

    $T_i / T_f = 1/4$

36. Find F_i / F_f

    $F = GMm / r^2$

    Mass 1 is doubled and the distance between the masses is tripled.

    Doubling the mass would double the force. Tripling the radius will cut the force by 1/9. So the new force is 2/9 of the old force:

    $F_i / F_f = 9/2$

37. Find F_i / F_f

    $F = GMm / r^2$

    Both masses are doubled and the distance between the masses is halved.

    $M_f = 2M_i$

    $m_f = 2m_i$

    $r_f = 2r_i$

    $F_i / F_f = (GM_im_i / r_i^2) / (GM_fm_f / r_f^2)$

    $= (M_im_i / r_i^2) / (M_fm_f / r_f^2)$

    $= (M_im_i / r_i^2) / (2M_i2m_i / [2r_i]^2)$

    $= (M_im_i / r_i^2) \times (4r_i^2 / 2M_i2m_i)$

    $= (1 / 1) \times (4 / 2 \times 2)$

    $= 1$

38. Find F_i / F_f

    $F = kQq / r^2$

    One charge is doubled, the other is halved, and the distance between the charges is doubled. Doubling one charge, Q, and halving the other charge, q, will cancel each other out. So the only change is doubling the distance, which will cut the force by a quarter:

    $F_i / F_f = 4/1$

39. If a sample of gas has the pressure and temperature held constant, but the volume doubles, then what must be true:

    (Use PV = nRT)

    If volume doubles, the left side of the equation doubles. To maintain the equality, the right side must also double. This means n doubles.

40. Solve for x: 2 log x = 10

    log x = 5

    $x = 10^5$

Section 3: Logarithms

Note: if no base is indicated, then it is the common log, $\log_{10}$

41. $\log_5 5 = 1$
42. $\log 1 = 0$
43. $\ln e = 1$
44. $2.3 \times \log_{10} e \approx 1$
45. $\log (3 \times 10^4) \approx \log 3 + \log 10^4 \approx 0.5 + 4 = 4.5$
46. $\log (X / Y) = \log X - \log Y$
47. $\log (1 / Q) = - \log Q$
48. $\log 100 = 2$
49. $\log 0.001 = -3$
50. $\log 10 = 1$
51. $\log (5 \times 10^5) \approx \log 5 + \log 10^5 = 0.7 + 5 = 5.7$
52. $-\log (2.5 \times 10^{-15}) \approx 15 - \log 2.5 = 14.7$
53. $-\log (10^5) = -5$
54. $-\log (8 \times 10^{-2}) \approx 2 - \log 8 \approx 1.2$
55. $\log 1/100 = \log 10^{-2} = -2$
56. $\log X^Y = Y \log X$
57. $\log 10^6 - \log 100,000 = 6 - 5 = 1$
58. $\log 50 + \log 2 = \log (50 \times 2) = 2$
59. $\log 4,000 - \log 40 = \log (4000 / 40) = 2$
60. $2 \times \log (\sqrt{10}) = \log (\sqrt{10})^2 = \log 10 = 1$

Section 4: Trig

61. $\sin 0° = 0$
62. $\cos 30° = \sqrt{3} / 2$
63. $\tan 45° = 1$
64. $\sin 60° = \sqrt{3} / 2$
65. $\cos 90° = 0$
66. $\tan 180° = 0$
67. $\sin 30° = 1/2$
68. $\cos 45° = \sqrt{2} / 2$
69. $\tan 60° = \sqrt{3}$
70. $\sin^{-1} 1/2 = 30°$
71. $\cos^{-1} 1/2 = 60°$
72. $\tan^{-1} 1 = 45°$
73. $\sin^{-1} \sqrt{3} / 2 = 60°$
74. $\cos^{-1} 0 = 90°$
75. $\tan^{-1} \sqrt{3} = 60°$
76. The hypotenuse of a 30-60-90 triangle is 4.2 meters long. The shorter leg is: 2.1 meters
77. One leg of a 45-45-90 triangle is 20 meters long. The other leg is: 20 meters
78. The longer leg of a 30-60-90 triangle is $\sqrt{6}$ meters long. The shorter leg is: $\sqrt{6} / \sqrt{3} = \sqrt{(6/3)} = \sqrt{2}$
79. The hypotenuse of a 45-45-90 triangle is $6\sqrt{2}$ meters long. The sum of the lengths of the legs is: 6+6 = 12
80. $(\sin 30°)^2 + (\cos 30°)^2 = 1$

Section 5: Units

Note: for the following, use the following conversion factors:

    1 yard = 3 feet = 36 inches
    1 inch = 2.5 cm
    1 Calorie = 1000 calories = 4184 J
    1 pound (lb) = 4.45 N

81. 15.2 cm in mm = 152
82. 1,500 μJ in kJ = 1500 x 10^{-6} J x 1 kJ / 10^3 J = 1500 x 10-9 kJ = 1.5 x 10^{-6} kJ
83. 3.2 Gg in kg = 3.2 x 10^3 kg
84. 0.0041 Ms in ms = 4.1 x 10^{-3} Ms x 10^6s / 1 Ms x 10^3 ms / 1 s = 4.1 x 10^6 ms
85. 2 m in inches = 200 cm x 1 in / 2.5cm = 80 in
86. 25 cm in inches = 25cm x 1 in / 2.5cm = 10 in
87. A garden is designed to be 2 yards long and 6 yards wide. How many square feet is this:

    6 feet x 18 feet = 108 ft²

88. An apartment is advertised as being 1881 square feet. This is how many square yards:

    1881 ft² x 1 yd / 3 ft x 1 yd / 3 ft = 1881 ft² x 1 yd² / 9 ft² = 209 yd²

89. A meal is advertised as containing 100 Calories. How many joules is this:

    100 Calories x 4184 J / 1 Cal = 418400 J = 4.184 x 10⁵ J

90. To boil a certain cup of water will take 836800 J of energy. How many calories is this:

    836800 J x 1 cal / 4.184 J = 200000 cal = 2 x 10⁵ cal

91. On earth, a person's weight is 100 pounds. On the moon, the person's weight in Newtons would be (approximate the gravitational force on the Moon as 1/5 that of Earth):

    100 pounds x 4.45N / 1 lb = 445 N
    445 N$_{EARTH}$ x 1/5 = 89 N$_{MOON}$

92. A bag of building materials weighs 8900 N. How many pounds is this:

    8900 N x 1 lb / 4.45 N = 2000 lb

93. An experiment is carried out at 298K. This is how many °C?

    25°C

94. The boiling point of water in F, °C, and K is:

    212F, 100°C, 373K

95. A car is able to drive 350 miles on a single tank of gas and the tank holds 15 gallons. How many miles per gallon does the car get:

    350 mi/tank x tank/15gal = 350/15 mi/gal = 70/3 = 23 1/3 mpg

96. A recipe calls for 10 g of flour and 20 g of sugar. A cook wishes to make 100 portions of this recipe. Flour is sold in 500g bags and sugar is sold in 250 g bags. The minimum number of bags of flour and sugar needed is:

    10g flour x 100 portions = 1000 g flour
    20g sugar x 100 portions = 2000g sugar
    1000g flour / 500g = 2 bags
    2000g sugar / 250g = 8 bags

97. 1 mile is 1.6 km and 1 gallon is 3.8 L. A car gets 40 miles per gallon. How many km per liter is this?

    40 mi/gal x 1.6km / 1mi x 1 gal/38L = 10x1.6/38 km/L = 16/38 = 8/19 km/L

98. A butterfly flies at 24 inches a second. How many meters per minute is this?

    24 in /sec x 60sec/1min x 2.5cm/1in x 1m/100cm = 24x60x2.5 / 100 = 36 m/min

99. The average adult human needs to consume 2000 Calories per day to maintain weight. How many joules per minute is this?

    2000 Cal/day x 4184 J / 1 Cal x 1 day / 24 hr x 1 hr / 60 min = 2000x4184 / 24 x 60 = 5811.1 J/min

100. The freezing point is: 32F, 0°C, 273K

Performance Analysis

90-100. Good job! Your math skills are solid. You can likely skip the math chapter, or perhaps just quickly review some of the questions that follow.

75-89. You got a large majority of the questions correct, but still hit enough trouble that you'll want to invest in a thorough review. Work your way through the math chapter, carefully review all of the questions, and then come back and re-do this assessment.

50-74. You hit some real trouble on this assessment. You'll need to work your way through the math chapter very slowly and carefully. Read it over more than once, make study sheets, and complete the questions at least twice. Then come back and re-take this assessment to make sure you've built up your skills to the point you need for Test Day.

<50. You're going to need heavy-duty review to get yourself ready for the MCAT, including work beyond this prep book. Consider picking up additional math review books to build up your fundamentals.

2. Arithmetic

The MCAT will expect you to be familiar with the foundational math operations covered in a typical pre-algebra level (ratios, percents, etc.) and then to apply those operations in a science context. If you're struggling with foundational pre-algebra math operations, you should pick up a math review book to cover those basics—something like an SAT or GRE review book would serve well here.

Estimation

The MCAT will reward an ability to get close to the right answer much more than getting the exact answer, simply because you'll get full credit in less time. When the answer choices are numbers, they are almost always spread out quite a bit. This gives us plenty of wiggle room to estimate quite a bit.

When doing estimation, you should generally try to make your estimations cancel each other out. So for example, if you were trying to estimate:

403.7 x 3.9 =

Here, if you round the 403.7 down to 400, you should round the 3.9 up to 4. That way, the effect of those roundings will cancel each other out:

403.7 x 3.9 ≈ 400 x 4 ≈ 1600

5021 x 312 / 1599

Here, if we want to round 5021 and 312 down to 5000 and 300, we should also round 1599 down to 1500. This gives us:

5021 x 312 / 1599 ≈ 5000 x 300 / 1500 ≈ 1500000 / 1500 ≈ 1000

Notice if, instead, we rounded the 1599 up to 1600 we would get:

5000 x 300 / 1600 = 937.5

This is almost twice as far from the right answer as our first estimate:

5021 x 312 / 1599 = 979.7

Before doing any rounding, you should also check the answer choices to see how far apart they are.

Probability and Statistics

The statistics you will see on the MCAT primarily revolve around two concepts: measures of central tendency and measures of variability. Measures of central tendency, such as mean, median, or mode, describe how a data set is clustered around its central data points. Measures of variability such as range and standard deviation tell us how tightly or loosely the data is clustered around those central points.

Mean

The mean is the arithmetic average of a set of data. You calculate the mean by adding up all of the numbers in the set and then dividing by the number of members in the set:

Mean = Sum of the values / Number of values

It is important to remember that the mean is not necessarily a number that's actually in the set. The mean can also be strongly influenced by a single very large or very small value. Consider the following examples:

Ages of people at John's retirement party: 53, 54, 56, 56, 61, 63, 65, 65

Mean = (53+54+56+56+61+63+65+65) / 8 = 473/8 = 59.125

Here, the average age is 59.125, which is not actually a number in the set. Now what if one of the attendees at the retirement part brought his granddaughter to the event?

Ages of people at John's retirement party: 1, 53, 54, 56, 56, 61, 63, 65, 65

Mean = (1+53+54+56+56+61+63+65+65) / 9 = 474/9 = 52.67

Here, a single data point—the one year old child—dragged the mean down to below every other person at the party.

So in the first example, the average age of about 59 was a good description of the people at the party—they were all folks who were right around 60 years old. In the second set, the mean isn't such a good description, because saying, "the average age at the party was in the low 50's" would not be an accurate description. The party consisted of people who were in their 50's to mid-60's. The tendency for the mean to be skewed by a small number of outlying data points often makes the median a better statistic to use.

Median

The median is the number that sits in the middle of a set of data when you arrange all of the numbers in a row. If there's an even number of data points, then the median is the arithmetic average of the two numbers that sit in the middle. Consider the examples from above:

Ages of people at John's retirement party: 53, 54, 56, 56, 61, 63, 65, 65

Here there are 8 data points. So you take the two numbers in the middle and average them:

Ages of people at John's retirement party: ~~53, 54, 56,~~ 56, 61, ~~63, 65, 65~~

Median = (56+61) / 2 = 117 / 2 = 58.5

When we add the 1 year old child we had:

Ages of people at John's retirement party: 1, 53, 54, 56, 56, 61, 63, 65, 65

Now there are 9 data points, so only one number sits in the middle:

Ages of people at John's retirement party: ~~1, 53, 54, 56,~~ 56, ~~61, 63, 65, 65~~

Median = 56

Notice that these two numbers are much closer together and more accurately reflect the age of the group even when the outlying data point of the 1 year old is considered.

Mode

The mode is the number that appears most frequently in a data set. There can be more than one mode, but if all numbers appear equally often, there is no mode. So for example:

Ages of people at John's retirement party: 1, 53, 54, 56, 56, 61, 63, 65, 65

Both 56 and 65 appear twice, so this is a set with two modes.

By contrast:

Ages of people at John's retirement party: 1, 53, 54, 56, 57, 61, 63, 65, 67

Now every single data point appears once, so there is no mode. One final example:

Ages of children on a little league team: 8, 9, 9, 9, 9, 9, 10, 10, 10, 10, 10, 11, 11, 11, 11, 11

In this set, the modes would be 9, 10, and 11. If the 8 were missing, there would be no mode.

The mode is a useful measure of the "average" of a set when the thing you're analyzing tends to happen very commonly at a certain point, and not very commonly at other times. For example, if you were analyzing the retirement age for police officers, the data set might look something like this:

Retirement age for police officers in a town: 55, 55, 55, 55, 55, 56, 56, 57, 70, 70

Mean: (55+55+55+55+55+56+56+57+70+70) / 10 = 584 / 10 = 58.4
Median: ~~55, 55, 55, 55,~~ 55, 56, ~~56, 57, 70, 70~~ = (55+56) / 2 = 55.5
Mode: 55

Here, the mode is 55 and that seems to be the best description. If you were to ask, "What's the normal or average age for a police officer to retire?" this data set would seem to suggest most police retire at 55.

There are a couple of folks who stayed on for another year or two and then two outliers who retired much older. That drags the average up to 58.4, but that number is misleading since it gives the impression that police officers wait until their late 50's to retire. The median is a better description at 55.5 but again it conveys the idea that what's "normal" or "average" is to wait past 55, whereas the data set much more clearly demonstrates that the typical police officer retires at 55.

Range

The range of a set is a fairly limited tool. You simply take the largest data point and subtract from it the smallest data point. It can give you a sense of how wide the extremes in the set are, but tells you very little beyond that.

Ages of people at John's retirement party: 53, 54, 56, 56, 61, 63, 65, 65

For this set, the range would be: R = 65 – 53 = 12

Ages of people at John's retirement party: 1, 53, 54, 56, 56, 61, 63, 65, 65

For this set, the range would be: R = 65 – 1 = 64

So certainly this measurement tells us that the second set has a much larger range.

Standard Deviation

Standard deviation is a measure of how spread out a data set is. The formula to calculate it is:

SD = √ [(Σ{xi – x]2) / (n – 1)]

Fortunately, you don't have to memorize this equation. All you have to know is that a bigger standard deviation means a set of data is more spread out, and a smaller standard deviation means a data set that is more clustered around the middle.

One relationship you should know is how a standard deviation relates to the normal bell curve distribution:

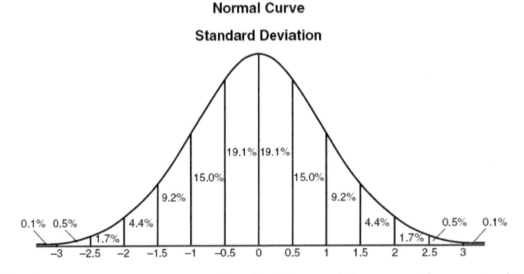

The normal distribution curve is an arrangement of data found in many different areas. If you were to plot out IQ scores, or MCAT scores, or the height of Americans, it would roughly form a normal distribution curve like this.

Here, "0" marks the mean of the data. Then each subsequent denotation is how many standard deviations away from the mean each part of the curve is. For the MCAT, you should know that 68.2% of the data points are going to lie within one standard deviation of the mean, that 95.4% are within two standard deviations, and 99.6% are within three standard deviations.

To put that in terms of the old MCAT scoring scale, in 2013 a score of about 25 was average on the 3 – 45 scale and the standard deviation was about 6 points. That meant that 2/3 of MCAT test takers scored in the range of 19 – 31 and over 95% of test-takers scored in the range of 13 – 37.

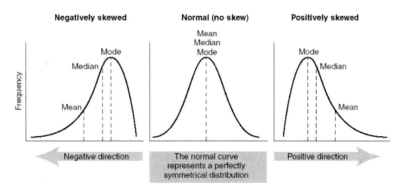

In addition to the normal distribution, the data set may also be skewed in one direction or another. If there are a lot of high-value outliers, the data set will be positively skewed. This pulls the mean up above the mode and median. An example might be income distribution in the US, with a smaller proportion of the population making much more money than is typical. Conversely, the data set might have more low-value outliers, giving a negatively skewed set. Those low-value data points will drag the mean down below the median and mode. An example might be the grades in a typical college biology 101 class: the bulk of students will get A's and B's, but a smaller fraction will bomb the class and those D's and F's will drag the average down.

Finally, a data set may represent two more common clusters of data. Such distribution is called bimodal:

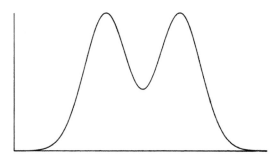

In this data set, there are two modes—two much more common outcomes, hence the name bimodal. An example might be how tall the average 90 year old is. The numbers will be quite different for men and women and so you will end up with two clusters—one for the average man and one for the average woman.

Percentile

A percentile is the percentage of data points falling below a given level. So, for example, imagine a class in which scores on a math test are as follows:

Math test scores: 43, 51, 69, 80, 81, 81, 81, 85, 85, 94

The person who scored a 43 on the test is at the 0th percentile. That is, 0% of the kids in the class scored below that person. The highest performing student—the one who got a score of 94 on the test, is at the 90th percentile. That is, 90 percent of the kids in the class scored below her. Notice that the range for percentiles is 0%ile to 99.9%ile. You cannot score 100th percentile because that would mean scoring higher than everyone (even yourself!)

To bring that back to the normal distribution curve, we can say that a data point that is 1 standard deviation above the norm would be the 84th %ile. We can get that number by adding up all of the percentages in the chart that are less than 1 standard deviation above the mean (15+19.1+19.1+15+9.2+4.4+1.7+0.5+0.1)

Inter-Quartile Range

Another way to measure the distribution in a data set is through the inter-quartile range. To do this, a data set is first split into quartiles. Much like finding the median, finding quartiles first involves arranging the data set in order, and then splitting it into fourths. For example, let's say a class of MCAT students gets the following scores on a practice test:

490, 492, 494, 494, 500, 500, 501, 502, 502, 503, 509, 519

To split the group into quarters we get:

490, 492, 494 || 494, 500, 500 || 501, 502, 502 || 503, 509, 519

Those groups are then named the first quartile, second quartile, and so on.

To find the interquartile range, we use the equation: $IR = Q_3 - Q_1$

To get the value of Q_1, we take the highest value in in the first quartile and the lowest value in the second quartile and average them. We do the same with the highest value in the third and lowest value in the fourth quartile to find Q_3. For example:

$Q_1 = (494 + 494) / 2 = 494$
$Q_3 = (502 + 503) / 2 = 502.5$

$IR = 502.5 - 494 = 8.5$

The IR then also gives us a specific mathematical definition of an outlier data point. Any score that is 1.5 IR's below Q_1 or 1.5 IR's above Q_3 is considered an outlier.

Here, the IR was 8.5, so the outliers would be 12.75 points below Q_1 or above Q_3. That is, any score below 481.25 or any score above 515.25 would be considered an outlier data point. In our set above, the only outlier is the one student who got a 519.

Probability

When calculating probability, we must first start with the probability of an individual event, X:

P_X = number of favorable outcomes in which X occurs / total number of possible outcomes

For example, the odds of rolling a standard 6-sided die and getting an even number (2, 4, or 6) is:

$P_{EVEN} = 3 / 6 = 1 / 2$

If two events are independent, then the probability of one event does not affect the probability of the other. Rolling two dice would be an example of this. However, if two events are dependent, then you must change the odds of the second event based on the outcome of the first.

When calculating the odds of two events both happening, simply multiply the two probabilities together. This can be a bit confusing since we use the word "and" in English but use multiplication when doing the math.

For example:

1. What are the odds of rolling two dice and getting a 2 on one and a 2 on the other?

$P_{\text{ROLL 2}} = 1 / 6$
$P_{\text{ROLL 2}}$ and $P_{\text{ROLL 2}} = 1/6 \times 1/6 = 1/36$

2. What the odds of flipping a coin three times and getting heads on all three flips?

P_{HEADS} and P_{HEADS} and $P_{\text{HEADS}} = 1/2 \times 1/2 \times 1/2 = 1/8$

When one event affects the other, you must account for that effect before multiplying the probabilities together:

1. A drawer has 10 white socks and 10 brown socks. What are the odds of drawing out a white sock and then another white sock?

$P_{\text{FIRST WHITE SOCK}} = 10 / 20$
$P_{\text{SECOND WHITE SOCK}} = 9 / 19$ (since we have already removed one white sock, there are only 9 white socks left and only 19 socks left in the drawer)

$P_{\text{BOTH WHITE SOCKS}} = (10 / 20) \times (9 / 19) = 90 / 380 = 9/38$

By contrast, when calculating the probability that one or the other of an event will occur, you must add the probabilities and then subtract the odds of them both happening. For example:

1. What are the odds of rolling at least one "2" on two six-sided dice?

$P_{\text{ROLL2}} = 1/6$
$P_{\text{ROLL2 TWICE}} = 1/36$
$P_{\text{ROLL2 ON EITHER}} = 1/6 + 1/6 - 1/36 = 11/36$

2. What are the odds of flipping heads on either of two fair coins?

$P_{\text{HEADS}} = 1/2$
$P_{\text{BOTH HEADS}} = 1/4$
$P_{\text{EITHER ONE IS HEADS}} = 1/2 + 1/2 - 1/4 = 3/4$

Finally, it is sometimes easier to calculate an event NOT happening and then using that to find the probability of an event happening. We must use:

$P_X + P_{\text{NOT X}} = 1$

For example:

1. The odds of rain are 20% each day for Monday, Tuesday, and Wednesday. What are the odds of rain on at least one day?

Here, the odds of no rain on a given day are 80% (remember X and Not X must add up to 1 or 100%). So the odds of no rain at all are:

$P_{\text{NO RAIN MONDAY}} \times P_{\text{NO RAIN TUESDAY}} \times P_{\text{NO RAIN WEDNESDAY}} = 0.8 \times 0.8 \times 0.8 = 0.512$

$P_{\text{NO RAIN AT ALL}} + P_{\text{RAIN AT LEAST ONCE}} = 1$

$P_{\text{RAIN AT LEAST ONCE}} = 1 - 0.512 = 0.488$

So there is a 48.8% chance of getting rain at least once.

2. What are the odds of flipping a coin five times and getting heads at least once?

Here, the odds of Not Heads is 1/2. To not get heads at least once means flipping the coin five times and getting tails every single time.

$P_{\text{NO HEADS, TAILS FIVE TIMES IN A ROW}} = 1/2 \times 1/2 \times 1/2 \times 1/2 \times 1/2 = 1/32$

$P_{\text{AT LEAST ONE HEAD}} + P_{\text{NO HEADS}} = 1$
$P_{\text{AT LEAST ONE HEAD}} = 1 - 1/32 = 31/32$

So, unsurprisingly, the odds of flipping a coin five times and getting heads one or more times is pretty high – 96.875%

Roots and Exponents

Manipulating roots and exponents is an essential part of doing MCAT math. Let's start with exponents.

There are a few key rules that we must memorize:

1. $N^0 = 1$

This is true for any number but 0. 0^0 is undefined and won't come up on the MCAT.

2. $N^X \times N^Y = N^{(X+Y)}$

A quick example can help show why this rule is true:

$5^2 \times 5^4 = (5 \times 5) \times (5 \times 5 \times 5 \times 5) = 5 \times 5 \times 5 \times 5 \times 5 \times 5 = 5^6 = 5^{(2+4)}$

3. $M^X \times N^X = (M \times N)^X$

Again, an example:

$2^3 \times 5^3 = 10^3 = 2 \times 2 \times 2 \times 5 \times 5 \times 5 = (5 \times 2) \times (5 \times 2) \times (5 \times 2) = (5 \times 2)^3 = 10^3$

4. $N^X / N^Y = N^{(X-Y)}$

For example: $5^5 / 5^2 = 5 \times 5 \times 5 \times 5 \times 5 / 5 \times 5 = 5 \times 5 \times 5 = 5^3 = 5^{(5-2)}$

5. $(N^X)^Y = N^{(X \times Y)}$

For example: $(5^2)^3 = 5^2 \times 5^2 \times 5^2 = 5^6 = 5^{(2 \times 3)}$

6. $(N/M)^X = N^X / M^X$

For example: $(2/3)^3 = (2^3) / (3^3) = 8 / 27$

7. $N^{(1/2)} = \sqrt{N}$

8. $N^{(-X)} = 1 / N^X$

In addition to knowing these eight rules, it can speed up your work tremendously and help you approximate to memorize the first twenty squares:

$1^2 = 1$	$5^2 = 25$	$9^2 = 81$	$13^2 = 169$	$17^2 = 289$
$2^2 = 4$	$6^2 = 36$	$10^2 = 100$	$14^2 = 196$	$18^2 = 324$
$3^2 = 9$	$7^2 = 49$	$11^2 = 121$	$15^2 = 225$	$19^2 = 361$
$4^2 = 16$	$8^2 = 64$	$12^2 = 144$	$16^2 = 256$	$20^2 = 400$

So if a question asks you to find the square root of 130, you likely won't need the exact number – you'll just need to know that it's between 11 and 12.

The two square root values that you must memorize are:
$\sqrt{2} \approx 1.4$
$\sqrt{3} \approx 1.7$

In terms of square root rules, simply apply the ones listed above for exponents. After all, a square root is just the exponent of 1/2 so all the rules listed above will apply to square roots as well.

Scientific Notation

Scientific notation is a way to manage numbers that would otherwise be so big or so small that working with them would be extremely clumsy

$3{,}141{,}500 = 3.1415 \times 10^6$

Here, we've taken a number and re-expressed it in terms of scientific notation. The 3.1415 is the **coefficient** and the 10^6 is the **exponent**. The coefficient must be a number between -10 and 10 (exclusive) and the exponent can be any integer. It's possible to express numbers in "sort of" scientific notation just for ease of calculation—having a coefficient that's bigger than 10 or an exponent that's a decimal, for example. We'll see some examples like that shortly.

For numbers less than 1, use a negative exponent. For example:

$0.0001415 = 1.415 \times 10^{-4}$

You can also adjust how a number is expressed in scientific notation to help with certain calculations. If you want to make the exponent bigger, make the coefficient smaller, and vice versa.

For example:

$2,300 = 2.3 \times 10^3 = 0.23 \times 10^4 = 23 \times 10^2$

Remember that if the exponent is negative, a "smaller negative" is a bigger number! For example:

$0.00023 = 2.3 \times 10^{-4} = 0.23 \times 10^{-3} = 23 \times 10^{-5}$

Now let's look at how to carry out basic operations using scientific notation.

Addition and Subtraction with Scientific Notation

To add or subtract two numbers that are expressed in scientific notation, first adjust them so that they have the same exponent. Then add the coefficients but don't change the exponent. For example:

$0.000034 + 0.0000091 =$
$3.4 \times 10^{-5} + 9.1 \times 10^{-6} =$
$34 \times 10^{-6} + 9.1 \times 10^{-6} =$
$43.1 \times 10^{-6} =$
4.31×10^{-5}

$45,000,000 + 6,700,000 =$
$4.5 \times 10^7 + 6.7 \times 10^6 =$
$4.5 \times 10^7 + 0.67 \times 10^7 =$
5.17×10^7

Multiplication, Division, and Roots with Scientific Notation

To multiply or divide numbers in scientific notation, simply multiply or divide the coefficients as you would any other numbers, and then follow the exponent rules discussed above for the exponents. Often it is helpful to separate the coefficients and exponents to keep track of what you're doing. For example:

$(3 \times 10^6) \times (4 \times 10^2) = 3 \times 4 \times 10^6 \times 10^2 = 12 \times 10^8 = 1.2 \times 10^9$

$(2 \times 10^{-3}) \times (7 \times 10^{-5}) = 2 \times 7 \times 10^{-3} \times 10^{-5} = 14 \times 10^{-8} = 1.4 \times 10^{-7}$

$(5 \times 10^{-8}) \times (5 \times 10^6) = 5 \times 5 \times 10^{-8} \times 10^6 = 25 \times 10^{-2} = 2.5 \times 10^{-1} = 0.25$

$(6 \times 10^8) / (1.5 \times 10^3) = (6 / 1.5) \times (10^8 / 10^3) = 4 \times 10^5$

$(3 \times 10^4) \times (6 \times 10^{-9}) / (9 \times 10^{-2}) = (3 \times 6 / 9) \times (10^4 \times 10^{-9} / 10^{-2}) = 2 \times 10^{-3}$

When taking the root of a number in scientific notation, the most important thing to do is adjust the number so that the exponent can easily be dealt with. Remember that taking the square root means cutting the exponent in half, taking the cube root means taking 1/3 of the exponent, and so on. For example:

$$\sqrt{(6.4 \times 10^9)} = \sqrt{(64 \times 10^8)} = \sqrt{64} \times \sqrt{10^8} = 8 \times 10^4$$

Significant Figures

The MCAT won't necessarily have questions that specifically test you on sig figs but you should generally be familiar with the rules:

1. Any number between the leftmost nonzero digit and the rightmost nonzero digit is significant.

So in the number 2300.02 all six of the digits are significant.

2. Zeroes are not significant if they are to the left of the leftmost nonzero digit.

So in the number 0045.2 the zeroes are not significant.

In the number 0.000403 the zeroes to the left of the four are not significant. The "4", "0", and "3" in a row are all significant.

3. Zeroes to the right of the rightmost nonzero digit are significant **only** if there is a decimal point.

So in the number 3020.00 all six digits are significant.

In the number 3020 the last zero on the right is **not** significant.

In the number 0.00012300 the 1, the 2, the 3, and the next two 0's are all significant.

4. When a number is being generated by a physical measurement in an experiment, the last digit is usually considered not significant since it's only an estimate.

Arithmetic Operations Practice Questions

1. 35.112 / 7.2 is closest to:
   A. 3
   B. 5
   C. 210
   D. 35000

2. 2.011 x 105 / 43 is closest to:
   A. 0.5
   B. 5
   C. 6.5
   D. 12

3. (29.8 + 115)/(144.4) is closest to:
   A. 0
   B. 1
   C. 30.5
   D. 31

4. A gumball dispenser has 40 red gum balls and 60 blue gum balls. The odds of two blue gum balls in a row is closest to:
   A. 6%
   B. 24%
   C. 36%
   D. 100%

5. A couple's genetic makeup means any girl they have has a 10% chance of being albino and any boy they have has a 20% chance of being albino. If they have one child, the odds of it being albino are:
   A. 5%
   B. 10%
   C. 15%
   D. 30%

6. In a normal deck of 52 cards, there are 13 cards of each suit (clubs, spades, hearts, diamonds). What are the odds of drawing a club from the deck, replacing the card, and then drawing another club?
   A. 1/4
   B. 13/52 x 12/51
   C. 1/16
   D. 1/4 + 1/4

7. $\sqrt{180}$ =
   A. $6\sqrt{5}$
   B. 14
   C. $9\sqrt{2}$
   D. $18\sqrt{10}$

8. How many significant digits are in the numbers 250.00, 35, and 0.0020, respectively?
   A. 3, 2, 4
   B. 2, 2, 4
   C. 2, 2, 2
   D. 5, 2, 2

9. $\sqrt{2.5 \times 10^{17}}$ =
   A. 1.4×10^{17}
   B. 6.25×10^{15}
   C. 2.5×10^{9}
   D. 5×10^{8}

10. $3 \times 10^{6} + 9 \times 10^{5}$ =
    A. 6×10^{5}
    B. 3.9×10^{6}
    C. 1.2×10^{6}
    D. 12×10^{11}

Arithmetic Operations Explanations

1. B.
Estimate as 35/7 = 5

2. B.
Estimate as 2 x 100 / 40 = 200/40 = 5

3. B.
Estimate as (30+115) / 145 = 1

4. C.
First blue gum ball = 60/100
Second blue gum ball = 59/99 (estimate as 60/100)

60/100 x 60/100 = 6/10 x 6/10 = 36/100 = 36%

5. C.
(50% $_{\text{CHANCE OF BOY}}$ x 10% $_{\text{ALBINO}}$)+ (50% $_{\text{CHANCE OF GIRL}}$ x 20% $_{\text{ALBINO}}$) = 15%

6. C.
Odds of drawing a club = 13/52 = 1/4

Replacing the card returns the deck to its original state, so the odds of the second club are also 1/4.

Odds of two clubs = 1/4 x 1/4 = 1/16

7. A.
Factor out:

$\sqrt{180} = \sqrt{(36 \times 5)} = \sqrt{36} \times \sqrt{5} = 6\sqrt{5}$

8. D.
The decimal makes the two zeros at the end of the 250 significant, so there are 5 sig figs in the first number. That makes the right answer D.

9. D.
Convert so the exponent is an even number, to make it easier to cut in half:

$\sqrt{(2.5 \times 10^{17})} = \sqrt{(25 \times 10^{16})} = \sqrt{25} \times \sqrt{10^{16}} = 5 \times 10^8$

10. B.
Convert so they both have the same exponent and then add the coefficients:

$3 \times 10^6 + 0.9 \times 10^6 = 3.9 \times 10^6$

3. Algebra and Trigonometry

You're going to see an awful lot of equations on the MCAT, and not just in the physics. The biology and biochemistry will give you experiments with all sorts of equations, and the general chemistry and organic chemistry have their equations as well. The MCAT typically won't ask you to solve equations in the way that a high school algebra class (or the GRE) would. But they will expect that you can do so, and they will then ask trickier, high-level relationship questions that presume that fundamental understanding. Run through the following chapter to brush up on your skills, and remind yourself of anything you might have forgotten.

Manipulating Equations

The MCAT will require you to be comfortable manipulating equations and variables roughly at the level of a high school Algebra I (or a little bit of Algebra II) course. To that end, we'll briefly review some foundational concepts here.

Direct and Inverse Relationships

Often the MCAT won't require you to solve for an exact number, if you can simply determine the relationship between the variables. They can either be direct or inverse. In a direct relationship, as one variable increases, the other increases as well. With inverse relationships, as one variable increases, the other goes down.

The equation for a direct relationship is:

$A \, / \, B = k$

where k is some constant. Alternatively, it could be presented as:

$A_1 \, / \, B_1 = A_2 \, / \, B_2$

A classic example of this kind of direct relationship is Charles's law, which states that temperature and volume of a gas are directly related:

$V_1 \, / \, T_1 = V_2 \, / \, T_2$

Inverse relationships are typically presented as:

$R \times Q = k$

$R_1 Q_1 = R_2 Q_2$

Again, a classic example of this is Boyle's law, which states that pressure and volume of a gas are inversely related:

$P_1 V_1 = P_2 V_2$

Graphically, these relationships typically look like this:

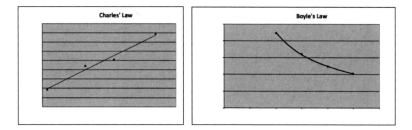

Systems of Equations

"Systems of equations" simply refers to situations in which you have two unknown variables and two different equations. To manipulate systems of equations on the MCAT, you will want to use substitution or combination. Let's consider the following two equations:

$2x + 9y = 31$

$3y - x = 7$

To solve, we can use either substitution or combination. Let's start with substitution. First, take one of the equations and isolate a variable. Let's take the second equation and isolate x:

$3y - x = 7$
$3y = 7 + x$
$3y - 7 = x$

Now we can substitute this value, $(3y - 7)$ into the first equation:

$2(3y - 7) + 9y = 31$
$6y - 14 + 9y = 31$
$15y - 14 = 31$
$15y = 45$
$y = 3$

Now that we know that y is three, we can plug that value back into one of the original equations:

$3(3) - x = 7$
$9 - x = 7$
$x = 2$

And so we have solved that x = 2 and y = 3.

To do combination, you will simply add the two equations together. For example, if you had the equations:

$3 \times 2 = 6$

$3 + 1 = 4$

You could add the left side of both equations and the right side of both equations and you'd still have a valid equation:

(3x2) + (3+1) = 6 + 4
6 + 4 = 10

And notice we still have a true equation at the end. For this process to be helpful with algebra, we will need one of the equations to cancel out one of the variables. In our first equation we had "2x" and in the second we had "-x". So make the x cancel out, multiply the second equation by 2:

3y – x = 7
2(3y – x) = 2(7)
6y – 2x = 14

We can now add the two equations together:

$$\begin{aligned} 2x + 9y &= 31 \\ + \; 6y - 2x &= 14 \end{aligned}$$

2x + 9y + 6y – 2x = 31 + 14
9y + 6y + 2x – 2x = 45
15y = 45
y = 3

And since we've done everything correctly, we arrive at the same answer as before – that y is three.

Trigonometry

As with so many other concepts on the MCAT, understanding trig starts with memorizing the basic concepts. Let's start with the definitions you'll be expected to know:

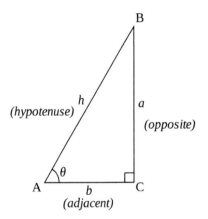

Sine:
sin θ = opposite / hypotenuse = a / h

Cosine:
cos θ = adjacent / hypotenuse = b / h

Tangent:
tan θ = opposite / adjacent = a / b

Inverse sine:
sin^{-1} (a/h) = arcsin (a/h) = θ

Inverse cosine:
cos^{-1} (b/h) = arccos (b/h) = θ

Inverse tangent:
tan^{-1} (a/b) = arctan (a/b) = θ

Rather than trying to calculate trig values, you should simply memorize the common values likely to show up on the MCAT. If you learn the following values, you'll be set for 99% of what you're likely to see on the MCAT:

sin 0° = √0 / 2 = 0
sin 30° = √1 / 2 = 1/2 = 0.5
sin 45° = √2 / 2 ≈ 0.7
sin 60° = √3 / 2 ≈ 0.87
sin 90° = √4 / 2 = 2/2 = 1
sin 180° = 0

Notice the pattern here – the denominator in each case is 2 and for the numerator you simply count up from 0 to 4 and take the square root.

cos 180° = 1
cos 90° = √0 / 2 = 0
cos 60° = √1 / 2 = 1/2 = 0.5
cos 45° = √2 / 2 ≈ 0.7
cos 30° = √3 / 2 ≈ 0.87
cos 0° = √4 / 2 = 2/2 = 1

Notice the pattern here – the denominator in each case is 2 and for the numerator you simply count up from 0 to 4 and take the square root.

tan 0° = 0
tan 30° = √3 / 3
tan 45° = 1
tan 60° = √3
tan 90° = undefined
tan 180° = 0

Unfortunately, there's not such an easy pattern for tangent!

Finally, the MCAT will expect you to have memorized the ratios between the sides for the 30-60-90 and the 45-45-90 right triangles. Here they are:

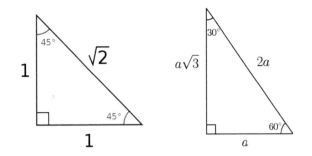

Logarithms

The MCAT includes a number of equations based on logarithms that you will be expected to use. For example:

pH = - log [H+]
$\Delta G = - RT \ln K_{eq}$

A logarithm is simply the inverse of an exponent. That is:

$10^A = B$
$\log_{10} B = A$

Since you will mostly be dealing with powers of ten, you should be very familiar with $\log_{10}$, and if no number is listed, simply assume that it is log base 10. You should also know the following:

log 0.01 = -2
log 0.1 = -1
log 1 = 0
log 3 ≈ 0.5
log 10 = 1
log 100 = 2

You won't be expected to calculate the exact value of log 2 through log 9, and usually on the MCAT you can simply estimate all of them as ≈0.5 (that is, just some value between 0 and 1).

The log rules you will need to know are:

1. $\log_X 1 = 0$
2. $\log_X X = 1$
3. log (N x M) = log N + log M
4. log (N / M) = log N – log M
5. $\log (N^M) = M \times \log N$
6. - log N = log (1 / N)

The only other log besides $\log_{10}$ you are likely to encounter on the MCAT is $\log_e$, or the natural log, ln. Euler's number, e, is about 2.7. You may find that you need to convert between $\log_{10}$ and ln, so use the following conversion:

$2.3 \times \log_{10} N = \ln N$

Log Scales: pH and Decibels

By far the two most common cases in which you will use log scales is when working with acid-base problems or with decibels. Remember that every "step" on a log scale means 10x more of whatever's being measured. So moving from pH 4 down to pH 3 means a solution that is ten times more acidic.

When solving for pH, use the following shortcut:

$$pH = -\log[H^+] = -\log[A \times 10^{-B}] = B - \log A$$

And remember we said that "log A" can simply be rounded off to 0.5 so long as A is a number between 1 and 10. For example, what is the pH of a solution whose $[H^+] = 4 \times 10^{-8}$?

$$pH = -\log[H^+] = -\log[4 \times 10^{-8}] = 8 - \log 4 \approx 7.5$$

The situation is slightly trickier with decibels (dB) since the decibel equation involves a ratio and puts a x10 into the equation itself:

$$dB = 10 \log(I / I_o)$$

For example, a 63 decibel sound is how much louder than a 23 decibel sound?

First, we see that this is a change of 40 decibels:

$$40 = 10 \log(I / I_o)$$
$$4 = \log(I / I_o)$$

The discussion of what I_o is and why the equation is set up as a ratio is beyond the scope of our discussion about log scales. For now, suffice to say that we see going from a 23 decibel sound to a 63 decibel sound involves 4 steps on a log scale—meaning the 63 decibel sound is 10^4 times louder. So the answer is, "The 63 decibel sound is ten thousand times louder (more intense) than the 23 decibel sound."

Algebra and Trigonometry Practice Questions

1. Solve for x: $3x / (x+2) = 5$
   A. 5
   B. -5
   C. -10
   D. -2

2. Solve for x:
   $2y - x = 5$
   $2x + 3y = 18$

   A. **A.** 3
   B. **B.** 4
   C. **C.** 4.5
   D. **D.** 14

3. Isolate log A: $pH = pKa + \log (A/HA)$
   A. $\log A = pH/pKa + \log HA$
   B. $\log A = pH - pKa + \log HA$
   C. $\log A = pH + pKa / \log HA$
   D. $\log A = \log HA (pH - pKa)$

4. $\sin 30° =$
   A. 0
   B. 1/2
   C. $\sqrt{2} / 2$
   D. 1

5. $\cos 180° =$
   A. 0
   B. - 1/2
   C. $\sqrt{2} / 2$
   D. - 1

6. $\tan 0° =$
   A. 0
   B. 1/2
   C. $\sqrt{2} / 2$
   D. 1

7. $\log_4 4 =$
   A. 0
   B. 1
   C. 4
   D. 512

8. $\log 25 + \log 4$
   A. 0
   B. 2
   C. 29
   D. 10^{29}

9. $\log (1/1000) =$
   A. 0.001
   B. 3
   C. -3
   D. -1000

10. $2 \log_5 \sqrt{5}$
    A. 1
    B. 2
    C. 5
    D. 25

Algebra and Trigonometry Explanations

1. B.
$3x / (x+2) = 5$
$3x = 5(x+2)$
$3x = 5x + 10$
$-2x = 10$
$x = -5$

2. A.
$2y - x = 5$
$2(2y - x = 5)$
$4y - 2x = 10$

$[4y - 2x = 10]$
$\underline{+[2x + 3y = 18]}$
$7y = 28$
$y = 4$

$2(4) - x = 5$
$8 - x = 5$
$x = 3$

3. B.
$pH = pKa + \log(A/HA)$
$pH - pKa = \log(A/HA)$
$pH - pKa = \log A - \log HA$
$pH - pKa + \log HA = \log A$

4. B.
Sine of 30° is 1/2.

5. D.
Cosine of 0° is 1 and cosine of 180° is -1.

6. A.
Tangent of 0° is 0.

7. B.
$\log_X X$ is always equal to 1.

8. B
$\log A + \log B = \log (A \times B)$
$\log 25 + \log 4 = \log (25 \times 4) = \log 100 = \log 10^2 = 2$

9. C
$-\log A = \log (1/A)$
$\log (1/1000) = - \log 1000 = - \log 10^3 = -3$

10. A
$2 \log_5 \sqrt{5} = \log_5 (\sqrt{5})^2 = \log_5 5 = 1$

4. Interpreting Graphs

Introduction

One of the most important skills you will need on Test Day is interpreting graphs and figures. The majority of the science passages you'll see on the MCAT will have some sort of table, graph, or figure with them. When you see any figures, you should always take a careful look at them as soon as you start your work on the passage. Focus on:

1. Title, Units, Axes, Labels

By far the most important thing to do when you see a figure is get yourself oriented to what it's even showing you. If it's a graph, what are the axes labeled? What are the units?

2. Trends

Are the numbers going up? Down? Random? What's the slope of the line if it's a graph?

3. Extremes, Outliers, Intercepts

If it's a graph, where does it intersect the x or y axis? Do the trend lines intersect at any point? Are there extremes? Big jumps in trends? Who's the biggest and smallest category?

4. What does the text say?

Finally, to pull it all together, you should see what the text has to say about the figure. Does it tell you something about the data in the figure? Does the data in the figure tell you something about the graph?

The Cartesian Plane

The basic coordinate system you will see on the MCAT will be the standard Cartesian plane, with a vertical y-axis and a horizontal x-axis. Units on the axes will typically be at standard intervals—each square will be 1 unit (for the sake of convenience, they may draw the graph with 1 square representing 5 units, 10 units, etc.)

To express information on a Cartesian plane, we use an ordered pair of coordinates, first listing the x coordinate and then the y coordinate. For example, in the graph below, the points (2, 3), (-5, 1), and (4, -2) have been plotted.

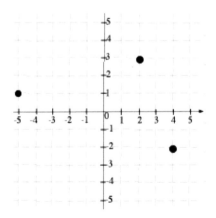

Linear Graphs

When representing data in a Cartesian plane, one of the most common forms you will see on the MCAT is a simple linear plot, with the classic formula structure y = mx+b. The m variable represents the slope:

m = slope = Δy / Δx

When analyzing a graph, remember that the units on the axes are important—the slope represents the units on the y-axis divided by the units on the x-axis. For example:

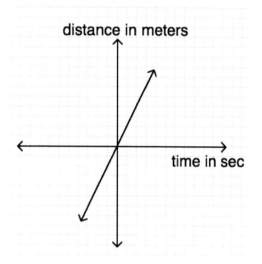

Here, we see a line that goes up by two units for every 1 unit along the x-axis. Thus its slope is 2 and the equation described by the line is d = 2t. The units for the slope would be m/s and so we can infer that the slope represents velocity.

In the y=mx+b formula, the "b" variable represents the y-intercept, the point at which the line crosses the y-axis. For example, in the following graph, the y-intercept is 2:

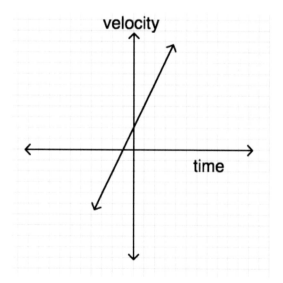

The slope is 2 and the y-intercept is 2, giving an equation y = 2x + 2. Since it is a graph of velocity vs. time the equation would be v = 2t+2 and the slope would represent (m/s)/s or m/s^2 which we can infer is acceleration.

Let's look at a couple of examples that would be linear based on some classic formulas you'd see on Test Day. The idea gas law is PV = nRT. If we graph this with PV on the y-axis and T on the x-axis we would get:

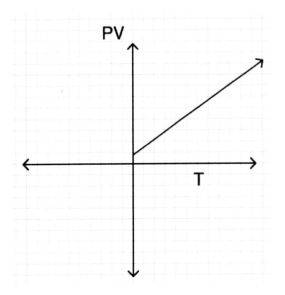

Here the line does not cross the y-axis into negative x values since temperature cannot be negative on the Kelvin scale. The slope of the line is "nR" and we remember that R is a constant and n is the number of moles of gas. So as temperature increases, the value of P x V increases linearly. The slope doesn't change at all because neither n nor R is changing.

In the kinematic equation $v_f = v_i + at$ we can see that v_f is the y-axis, t is the x-axis, a is the slope, and v_i is the y-intercept. Such a graph would look like the velocity vs. time graph depicted above.

Conic Sections

The MCAT will also present you with many relationships that are not just straight lines. Most commonly, you'll see parabolic relationships, exponential relationships, and logarithmic ones. Here's a quick look at what they look like.

Here's a graph of the exponential relationship $y = 10^x$

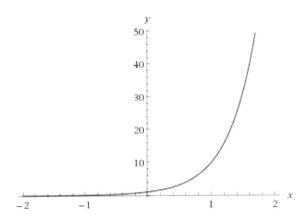

You see this kind of exponential curve in the Arrhenius equation: $k = Ae^{-Ea/RT}$ if you were to plot the rate constant k vs. the exponent E_a/RT.

In a parabola, the dependent variable changes as the square (or cube, etc.) of the independent variable. The classic example is $y = x^2$ and the graph looks like this:

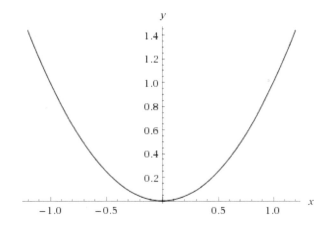

This parabolic relationship would be seen in the kinetic energy equation, for example, $KE = (1/2)mv^2$ if you were to plot KE versus velocity.

Finally, in a logarithmic relationship of $y = \log x$, y increases quickly at first but then slows down dramatically:

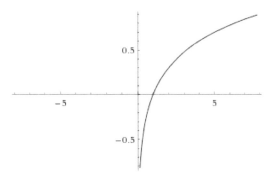

The classic example of this would be the pH or decibel scales, $pH = -\log[H^+]$ and $dB = 10 \log I$.

Semilog and Log-Log Scales

The MCAT will also give you graphs in which the x and y axes are not labeled in a linear fashion, which each box on the graph representing 1 unit, but rather the distance between the boxes representing a fixed ratio—that is, each line on the graph is ten times more than the one before it.

In a semilog graph, the y-axis is graphed in this ratio fashion while the x-axis is still labeled a unit at a time. Data is graphed this way when the value on the y-axis increases very quickly, and graphing it in a regular linear plot would be unwieldy. For example, imagine a graph of the mass of bacteria growing in a colony (measure in μg) plotted vs. time. The graph would increase very slowly at first, but would grow very rapidly as the colony keeps doubling over and over. On a simple linear plot the graph would shoot off the top of the chart pretty quickly, but in a semilog plot it might look like this:

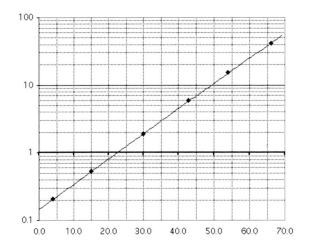

You may also see a log-log plot on the MCAT, although this is much less likely. In a log-log plot, both the x and y axes are listed as a constant ratio between segments, rather than a constant interval:

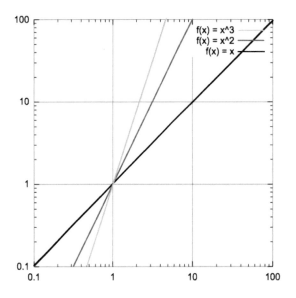

Other Charts and Graphs

Pie Charts

Pie charts are used to represent parts of a whole—the entire circle must represent 100% or the total number of data points. Pie charts are popular when showing demographic or epidemiological data. Their value lies in providing a quick, visually intuitive way to represent how much a total is made up of various groups (how big a "piece of the pie" each group takes). To be useful, however, the number of categories expressed in the pie must be relatively small. Compare the two pie charts below. In the first, the data is clear and easy to understand, but in the second the large number of categories makes the chart much less helpful.

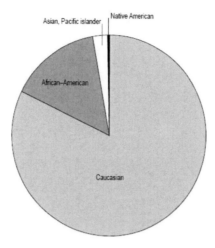

Figure 1F. Racial breakdown of population of Indiana

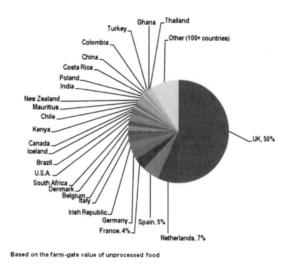

Figure 2F. Country of Origin for Food consumed in the UK

Bar Graphs

Bar graphs present data sorted by category. They allow for quick comparison across groups. One type of bar graph is a histogram, in which the categories are various numerical values or ranges. For example, the chart below is a histogram of MCAT Verbal Reasoning Scores from the 2013 test administrations.

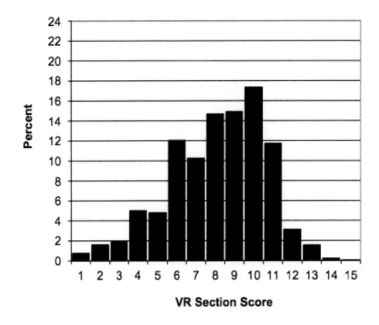

VR Section Score

Box-and-Whisker Plot

In a box-and-whisker plot data is graphed to show several things at once. The bottom edge of the box is the 25th %ile, the top edge of the box is the 75th %ile, the line in the middle of the box is the median, and the whiskers extend out to the minimum and maximum values in the data set.

Number of disciplinary infractions by grade

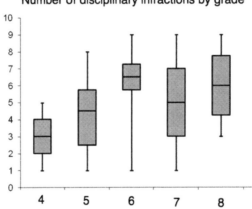

Other Representations of Data

Data may, of course, also be represented in any number of other ways. Symbols may be used to represent numbers in any way that makes it more visually compelling and easy to understand at a glance. For example, showing data spread out geographically can also provide quick, useful information.

Interpreting Graphs Practice Questions

Questions 1-2 use the following graph:

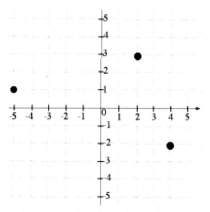

1. What is the slope of a line connecting the points (2, 3) and (4, -2)?
    A. -2.5
    B. -0.4
    C. 0.4
    D. 2.5

2. What is the slope of a line connecting the points (-5, 1) and (2, 3)?
    A. -7/2
    B. -2/7
    C. 2/7
    D. 7/2

Questions 3-5 use the following graph:

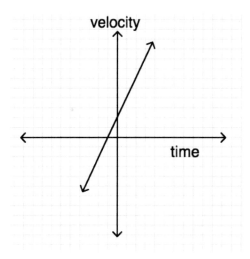

3. If each vertical unit on the graph represents 5 m/s and each horizontal unit represents 1 s then this object has a v_i of:
   A. 2 m/s
   B. 5 m/s
   C. 10 m/s
   D. 10 m/s^2

4. If each vertical unit on the graph represents 5 m/s and each horizontal unit represents 1 s then this object has an acceleration of:
   A. 1 m/s^2
   B. 5 m/s^2
   C. 10 m/s^2
   D. 25 m/s^2

5. If each vertical unit on the graph represents 5 m/s and each horizontal unit represents 1 s then from t=0 to t=3 the total distance covered by this object is:
   A. 15 m
   B. 39 m
   C. 45 m
   D. 75 m

Questions 6-8 use the following graphs:

Graph I:

Graph II:

Graph III:

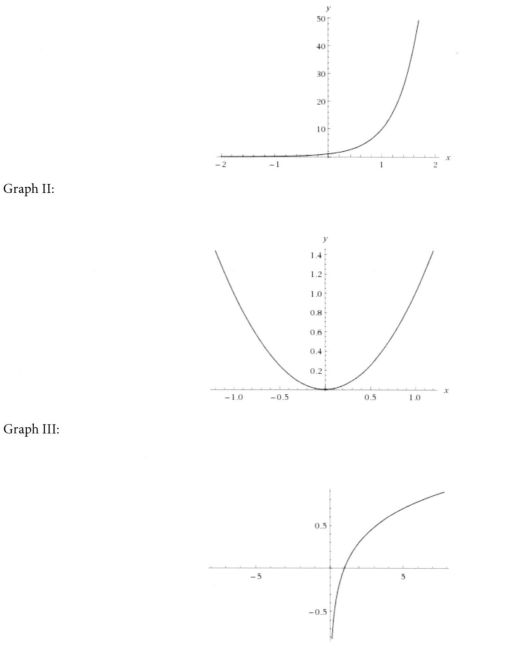

6. Which of the graphs above represents an exponential relationship?
    A. I
    B. II
    C. III
    D. None

7. Which of the graphs above would best represent the relationship $d = v_f^2/2a$ if d were graphed on the y axis and v_f on the x axis?
   A. I
   B. II
   C. III
   D. None

8. Which of the graphs above would best represent the binding curve for hemoglobin and oxygen *in vivo*?
   A. I
   B. II
   C. III
   D. None

Questions 9-10 use the following graph:

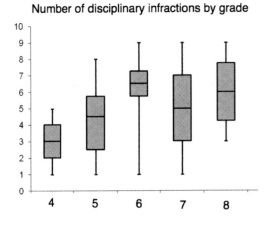

9. The data set for which grade shows the largest range?
   A. 4
   B. 5
   C. 6
   D. 7

10. The data set for which grade shows a 25th and 75th percentile that are the closest together?
    A. 4
    B. 5
    C. 6
    D. 7

Interpreting Graphs Explanations

1. A.
Slope = $\Delta y / \Delta x = 3 - (-2) / 2-4 = 5 / -2 = -2.5$

2. C.
Slope = $\Delta y / \Delta x = 1 - 3 / -5 - 2 = -2 / -7 = 2/7$

3. C.
The initial velocity will be where t=0 which is the y-intercept on this graph. The y-intercept is two boxes up on the graph and the question tells us that each one is 5 m/s. So the v_i is 10 m/s.

4. C.
Acceleration is m/s / s or m/s^2. On this graph, acceleration is represented by the slope of the line. The line slopes up 2 units for every 1 unit over. That's 10 m/s up and 1 sec over, for an acceleration of $a = 10$ m/s $/ 1 s = 10 m/s^2$

5. C.
Distance is measured in meters. The vertical axis is m/s and the horizontal is in sec. To find meters, we multiply them together—that is, we must find the area under the curve to get the total meters travelled. The shape under the curve consists of a rectangle with dimensions 10x3 (for an area of 30) and a triangle with dimensions 15x6 (for an area of 45). Thus the total area under the curve is 75. (Remember the y-axis is 5 m/s per line)

6. A.
Graph I represents the curve of the line $y = 10^x$, which is an exponential relationship.

7. B.
Graph II represents the curve of the line $y = x^2$ which is the kind of parabola that would be described by the equation in the question.

8. D.
Hemoglobin binding to oxygen is a sigmoidal curve, and none of the graphs presented are sigmoidal.

9. C.
In a box-and-whisker plot, the outer edges of the whiskers indicate the range of the data. Here, the grade 6 had the widest whiskers, indicating the largest range in number of disciplinary infractions.

10. C.
In a box-and-whisker plot, the top and bottom edges of the box indicate the 75th and 25th percentiles. Thus the smallest box would indicate the 75th and 25th percentiles that are the closest together. Here, the smallest box is for grade 6.

5. Units

The MCAT will expect you to be familiar with a wide array of metric units. The good news is that most of these will be very familiar from your previous class work. The unit conversions discussion at the end is especially important, as converting between units is a skill tested on all of the science sections. Be sure to get in plenty of practice, and always be mindful of the units as you do your problem solving.

Units to Know

The SI system has both base and derived units. You should be familiar with all of the base units and the derived units listed here.

SI Base Units

UNIT	SYMBOL	QUANTITY MEASURED
meter	m	length
kilogram	kg	mass
second	s	time
ampere	A	current
kelvin	K	temperature
mole	mol	amount of substance
candela	cd	luminosity

SI Derived Units

UNIT	SYMBOL	DERIVATION	QUANTITY MEASURED
hertz	Hz	s^{-1}	frequency
newton	N	$kg \cdot m \cdot s^{-2}$	force
pascal	Pa	$kg \cdot m^{-1} \cdot s^{-2}$	pressure
joule	J	$kg \cdot m^2 \cdot s^{-2}$	energy
watt	W	$kg \cdot m^2 \cdot s^{-3}$	power
coulomb	C	$s \cdot A$	charge
volt	V	$kg \cdot m^2 \cdot s^{-3} \cdot A^{-1}$	potential, emf
farad	F	$kg^{-1} \cdot m^{-2} \cdot s^4 \cdot A^2$	capacitance
ohm	Ω	$kg \cdot m^2 \cdot s^{-3} \cdot A^{-2}$	resistance
tesla	T	$kg \cdot s^{-2} \cdot A^{-1}$	magnetic field strength
degree Celsius	°C	K	temperature

Conversions

Converting between metric units starts with knowing the prefixes used in the metric system. They are:

EXPONENT	PREFIX	ABBREVIATION
10^{12}	tera	T
10^9	giga	G
10^6	mega	M
10^3	kilo	k
10^2	hecta	h
10^1	deka	da
10^{-1}	deci	d
10^{-2}	centi	c
10^{-3}	milli	m
10^{-6}	micro	μ
10^{-9}	nano	n
10^{-12}	pico	p

When converting from one metric unit to the next, start by expressing the number in base units and then convert to the new prefix. Here are some examples:

1200 kJ is how many mJ?
1200 kJ = 1200×10^3 J
1200×10^3 J x (1 mJ / 10^{-3} J) = 1200×10^6 mJ = 1.2×10^9 mJ

62 Gm is how many km?
62 Gm = 62×10^9 m
62×10^9 m x (1 km / 10^3 m) = 62×10^6 km = 6.2×10^7 km

405 mΩ is how many MΩ?
405 mΩ = 405×10^{-3} Ω
405×10^{-3} Ω x (1 MΩ / 10^6 Ω) = 405×10^{-9} MΩ = 4.06×10^{-7} MΩ

Converting between English and Metric

The MCAT won't expect you to memorize English units, but it may provide you with the conversion factor and then ask you to convert between them. The only conversion factor you should memorize is between temperature scales—Fahrenheit to Celsius to Kelvin.

You should, however, be familiar with the general scale of these conversions so you know if your answers make sense as you solve questions:

BASE UNIT	EQUIVALENT UNIT	METRIC UNIT
1 mile	5280 feet, 1760 yards	1.6 km
1 foot	12 inches	30.48 cm
1 inch	1/12 foot	2.54 cm
1 Calorie	1000 calories	4184 J
1 pound	16 ounces (oz)	4.45 N
1 gallon	4 quarts, 16 cups, 128 fluid oz	3.79 L

Temperature conversions

Converting between Celsius and Kelvin is easy enough—simply take the Kelvins and subtract 273 to get the Celsius value. Converting between Celsius and Fahrenheit is a little more complex, using the formula below:

$F = (9/5)C + 32$

$C = K - 273.15$

TEMPERATURE	FAHRENHEIT	CELSIUS	KELVIN
Water freezing	32 F	0°C	273 K
Standard Conditions	77 F	25°C	298 K
Water boiling	212 F	100°C	373 K

Dimensional Analysis

One of the most important skills you can bring with you into the room on Test Day is a mastery of the relationships between SI units, and an ability to manipulate the units given in a problem or passage. Many times, even if you forget the equation, or can't figure out what's going on in the passage, if you "make the units work" you can get the right answer.

For example, if you were given a problem which said that a machine which does 150 watts of work operates for 10 seconds at a potential of 5 volts, and then asks you how many coulombs of charge were moved, you may not be sure what equation, if any, applies to this situation. However, if you remember the unit conversions:

Volt = Joule / Coulomb

Watt = Joule / s

You can use those unit conversions to find the answer:

$V = J/C$
$W = J/s$
$J = VC = Ws$

$VC = Ws$
$(5V)(C) = (150W)(10s)$
$C = 300$ coulombs

Next, a common issue in dimensional analysis is converting between units when one of the units is squared or cubed. When doing so, be sure to apply the conversion as many times as needed to get the desired units at the end. Here are a couple of examples:

10 m^2 is how many cm^2?

10 m^2 x (100 cm / 1 m) x (100 cm / 1 m) =

10 m^2 x (10000 cm^2 / 1 m^2) =

100000 cm^2

1,500 mL is how many m^3?

1,500 mL x (1 cm^3 / 1 mL) = 1,500 cm^3

1,500 cm^3 x (1 m / 100 cm) x (1 m / 100 cm) x (1 m / 100 cm) =

1,500 cm^3 x (1 m^3 / 10^6 cm^3) = 1,500 x 10^{-6} m^3 = 1.5 x 10^{-3} m^3

Finally, dimensional analysis can lead you to the right answer even in cases where the discussion in the passage doesn't relate to typical SI or English units, and for which there is no equation. Simply set up the conversion with the units in the answer choices in mind, and then apply whatever conversions you're given to make the remaining units cancel out. Here are a couple of examples with nonsense units:

A woman has 6 zops. Every 2 zops are worth 3 square zaps and a single zap is only worth 1/5 of a zip. How many square zips does she have?

The conversions they gave us: 2 zop / 3 zap^2 and 5 zaps / 1 zip

To convert zops to zip^2:

6 zop x (3 zap^2 / 2 zops) x (1 zip / 5 zap) x (1 zip / 5 zap) =

6 zop x (3 zap^2 / 2 zops) x (1 zip^2 / 25 zap^2) =

6x3/2x25 zip^2 = 18 / 50 = 36/100 = 0.36 zip^2

A man has a freeble that holds 12 plunks. The going rate is five dollars a plunk. The man has 6 dups that he can sell and he knows he can get $20 per dup. If he sells all of his dups how many times can he fill the freeble with plunks?

The conversions they gave us: 1 freeble / 12 plunk, 1 plunk / $5, 1 dup / $20, and that the man has 6 dups

To find how many freebles he can get:

(1 freeble / 12 plunk) x (1 plunk / $5) x ($20 / 1 dup) x 6 dup = 2 freebles

Units Practice Questions

1. Which of the following is equal to a joule?
   A. $kg \cdot m^2 \cdot s^{-1}$
   B. $kg \cdot m \cdot s^{-2}$
   C. $N \cdot m^{-1}$
   D. $W \cdot s$

2. The SI unit for charge is divided by the SI unit for current. This gives:
   A. time.
   B. volt.
   C. electron-volt.
   D. force.

3. 3.21 g is how many kg?
   A. 0.00321
   B. 0.0321
   C. 3.21
   D. 3210

4. 642 GJ is how many nJ?
   A. 6.42×10^{-18}
   B. 6.42×10^{11}
   C. 6.42×10^{18}
   D. 6.42×10^{20}

5. A Fahrenheit scale reads -40°F. This is how many °C?
   A. -72 °C
   B. -40 °C
   C. -22.2 °C
   D. -8 °C

6. Standard thermodynamic conditions are P = 1 atm and T = 298 K. This is what temperature in Celsius?
   B. 0 °C
   B. 25 °C
   C. 77 °C
   D. 298 °C

For questions 7-8 use the following conversions:
1 inch = 2.5 cm
1 cal = 4.184J

7. A meal is advertised as containing 963 kcal. How many joules is this?
   A. 4.03×10^{-6} J
   B. 3,891 J
   C. 963,000 J
   D. 4,029,192 J

8. A particular fabric is sold at $1 for every ten square inches. Which of the following is closest to the cost of two thousand square centimeters, at this rate?
   A. $0.30
   B. $3
   C. $30
   D. $300

9. A person runs at 1.5 m/s and her strides are 0.75 m long. The track she is walking around is 150 meters long. Approximately how many strides will it take her to complete a loop around the track?
   A. 100 strides
   B. 112.5 strides
   C. 150 strides
   D. 205 strides

10. A person runs at 1.5 m/s and her strides are 0.75 m long. The track she is walking around is 150 meters long. How long will it take her to complete a loop around the track?
    A. 100 s
    B. 112.5 s
    C. 150 s
    D. 225 s

Units Explanations

1. D.
A watt is a joule per second, so a joule is a watt times a second.

2. A.
Current, amps, can be expressed as charge per time, coulombs / seconds.

Amp = Coul / sec

Rearranging this equation we get:

sec = Coul / Amp

Thus charge divided by current gives time.

3. A.
$3.21g \times (1 \text{ kg} / 10^3 \text{ g}) = 3.21 \times 10^{-3} \text{ kg} = 0.00321 \text{ kg}$

4. D.
$642 \text{ GJ} \times (10^9 \text{ J} / 1 \text{ GJ}) \times (10^9 \text{ nJ} / 1 \text{ J}) = 642 \times 10^{18} \text{ nJ} = 6.42 \times 10^{20} \text{ nJ}$

5. B.
$F = (9/5)(°C) + 32$
$-40 = (9/5)(°C) + 32$
$-72 = (9/5)(°C)$
$(-72)(5/9) = °C$
$-40 = °C$

6. B.
$K = °C + 273$
$298 = °C + 273$
$25 = °C$

7. D.
963 kcal x (1000 cal / 1 kcal) x (4.184 J / 1 cal) = 4,029,192 J

Note that you can estimate this as 1000 x 4000 to see that the answer will be around 4 million, which is enough to get the question right.

8. C.
$1 / 10 \text{ in}^2$ x (1 in / 2.5 cm) x (1 in / 2.5 cm) x 2000 cm^2 = \$32. This is closest to choice C.

9. D.
150m x (1 stride / 0.75 m) = 200 strides. This is closest to choice D.

10. A.
150m x (1 s / 1.5 m) = 100 s